The Latin American Studies Book Series

The Latin American Studies Book Series promotes quality scientific research focusing on Latin American countries. The series accepts disciplinary and interdisciplinary titles related to geographical, environmental, cultural, economic, political, urban and health-related research dedicated to Latin America. The series publishes comprehensive monographs, edited volumes and textbooks refereed by a region or country expert specialized in Latin American studies.

The series aims to raise the profile of Latin American studies, showcasing important works developed focusing on the region. It is aimed at researchers, students, and everyone interested in Latin American topics.

Submit a proposal: Proposals for the series will be considered by the Series Advisory Board. A book proposal form can be obtained from the Publisher, Andrea Brody-Barre (andrea.brody-barre@springer.com).

Antonio di Campli
Editor

Inhabiting Debt

Ecologies of Dependance and Resistance in Latin America

Springer

Editor
Antonio di Campli
DIST, Interuniversity Department of Urban and Regional Studies and Planning
Politecnico di Torino
Torino, Torino, Italy

ISSN 2366-3421 ISSN 2366-343X (electronic)
The Latin American Studies Book Series
ISBN 978-3-031-99885-0 ISBN 978-3-031-99886-7 (eBook)
https://doi.org/10.1007/978-3-031-99886-7

This Springer imprint is published by the registered company Springer Nature Switzerland AG
The registered company address is: Gewerbestrasse 11, 6330 Cham, Switzerland

To those who inhabit debt as a condition inscribed in space, who navigate its constraints as one moves through a city—finding paths, forging crossings, resisting enclosure.
To those who transform precarity into solidarity, extraction into organization, vulnerability into collective strength.
To those who build cities that are not merely infrastructures of capital, but spaces of life, resistance, and possibility.
To those who read the city not as a neutral territory, but as a battlefield where relations of power are inscribed in space.
To those who read in the fractures not absence but unfinished work, in the margins not periphery but potential, in the unbuilt not failure but the architecture of what is yet to come.

Foreword

Debt is not a transaction. It is not an agreement between equals, nor a neutral instrument of exchange. Debt is a relation of force, a mechanism of discipline, a slow violence inscribed in space. It is control: a way of governing populations, regulating desires, containing futures. It dictates what is possible and what is not, who may inhabit a space and under what conditions, who must remain trapped in the endless cycle of repayment.

It is not abstract; it is brick, concrete, and asphalt.

It thickens the air of the neighborhoods it builds, the rooms it expands, the windows it leaves unfinished. Debt constructs cities, but only by constraining their inhabitants, binding their futures to the weight of accumulated obligations.

There is no economy without space, just as there is no space that is not already shaped by economic imperatives. To separate the two is a fiction, and a dangerous one. Indebtedness is not simply a financial condition; it is a spatial order, a social structure, a way of dwelling and working. To be in debt is to negotiate with walls that were never meant to shelter but to extract value, to inhabit a house that is also a contract, a promise made under duress. And yet, those who are most burdened by debt also become its architects: enlarging homes, housing generations under the same precarious roof, opening small shops, adding floors to a life that remains unfinished. They transform what was imposed upon them into something of their own, despite everything.

But debt is never total. Within its constraints, through its very mechanisms, strategies of resistance emerge. The same structures designed to discipline—contracts, mortgages, loans—become spaces of negotiation, of subversion. The logic of debt demands obedience, but debtors rewrite its terms in increments of concrete and paint, in clandestine extensions, in informal economies woven into the fabric of the city. Debt may govern, but it does not control entirely. It is a site of struggle, an arena where survival and refusal take material form.

Women know this best. Not only because they are overrepresented in these economies of debt, but because they are the ones who sustain them—accountants of the impossible, balancing loans with survival, mortgages with meals, interest payments with the needs of those they care for. Without them, debt would collapse under its own weight. But it does not collapse. It reproduces itself, expands, demands more.

What does it mean, then, to think of debt as a spatialized practice? Not only to document its effects, but to recognize its projective force, its power to determine the material and social shape of the city. To study debt is to study a process that does not end: a city that is never finished, a home that is never complete, a life always lived in the shadow of what is owed. But it is also to ask whether things could be otherwise.

In this sense, this book offers a way to think about space, debt, and urbanization in a way that is operative, that can inform planning and design. It invites architects, urbanists, and policymakers to reconsider the role of financialization in shaping the city and to imagine new ways of intervening—ways that do not merely accommodate debt, but challenge its most perverse effects, reclaiming space as a common good rather than a financial asset.

This book does not offer reassurance. It does not suggest that the structures it describes can be easily reformed. Instead, it forces us to confront a question that has long been avoided: what kind of city do we build when debt is its foundation? And what forms of collective action might reclaim space from the financial logics that govern it?

The answers are not given. But they are urgently needed.

Antonio di Campli
DIST, Interuniversity Department of Urban and Regional Studies and Planning
Politecnico di Torino
Torino, Torino, Italy

Competing Interests

The editor and authors of the chapters included in this volume declare that they have no financial, institutional, or personal conflicts of interest that could have influenced the selection, editing, or publication of this volume.

Ethics Approval

This work has been carried out in line with international standards for responsible research publication.

The studies have been performed in accordance with the ethical standards as laid down in the 1964 Declaration of Helsinki.

Acknowledgments

This work emerges from the intersection of theoretical reflections and concrete struggles that shape urban space and the lives of those who inhabit it. It is indebted to those who refuse to see the city as a neutral composition of forms and functions, instead revealing it as a contested terrain where debt, capital, and power inscribe themselves onto the built environment.

Gratitude is owed to the subjects, communities, and collectives that, in cities and peripheries around the world—from the popular settlements of Andean medium-sized cities such as Loja to the contested neighborhoods of Quito—transform indebtedness into a terrain of struggle and political experimentation. To those who reclaim housing as a right rather than a commodity, who contest the extractive logic of real estate speculation, and who reimagine urban space not as a mechanism of accumulation but as a commons in the making.

Thanks are extended to the women who sustain popular and domestic economies, making visible the invisible labor upon which financial capitalism rests. To those who resist displacement and dispossession, not only by defending what remains but by envisioning what could be.

Gratitude is also extended to those who, within and beyond academia, continue to interrogate the relationship between space and power, rejecting the ideology of neutral planning and constructing counter-narratives and counter-spaces. To those who, against the violence of technocratic urbanism, persist in the belief that another city—another way of inhabiting the world—is still possible.

Finally, I express my deep gratitude to my colleagues in Quito and Loja, who generously devoted their time and energy to this research and publication. Without their support, this work would not have been possible.

Contents

Editor and Contributors

About the Editor

Antonio di Campli is Associate Professor in Urban Planning at the Polytechnic of Turin, Interuniversity Department of Regional and Urban Studies and Planning (DIST), Italy. He has been Professor and developed research activities in various universities in Italy, Switzerland, Colombia, and Ecuador. His research interests lie at the intersection of urban studies, urban planning, and the social sciences, and concern issues of "coexistence of differences," conflicts, and interactions between ecologies, economies, and practices of spatial production, investigated mainly through decolonial and Southern epistemologies.

Contributors

David Pazmiño Amaya International University of Ecuador (UIDE), Business School, Quito, Ecuador

Andrea Pacheco Barzallo Faculty of Arts, Design and Architecture, International University of Ecuador (UIDE), Quito, Ecuador

Rebeca Gallegos Bustamante Faculty of Arts, Design and Architecture, International University of Ecuador (UIDE), Quito, Ecuador

Marco Lenin Lara Calderón Faculty of Arts, Design and Architecture, International University of Ecuador (UIDE), Quito, Ecuador

Antonio di Campli DIST, Interuniversity Department of Urban and Regional Studies and Planning, Politecnico di Torino, Torino, Torino, Italy

Andrea Ordoñez León Faculty of Arts, Design and Architecture, Universidad Internacional del Ecuador (UIDE), Loja, Ecuador

Mauricio Unda Padilla Faculty of Arts, Design and Architecture, International University of Ecuador (UIDE), Quito, Ecuador

Claudia Costa-De los Reyes Faculty of Arts, Design and Architecture, Universidad Internacional del Ecuador (UIDE), Loja, Ecuador

Patricio Andino Sosa International University of Ecuador (UIDE), Business School, Quito, Ecuador

Verónica Muñoz-Sotomayor Faculty of Arts, Design and Architecture, Universidad Internacional del Ecuador (UIDE), Loja, Ecuador

María Fernanda León Vivanco Faculty of Arts, Design and Architecture, Universidad Internacional del Ecuador (UIDE), Loja, Ecuador

Abbreviations

AID	Agency for International Development
BEV	Banco Ecuatoriano de la Vivienda (Ecuadorian Housing bank)
EAFF	Encuesta Activos FLACSO-Florida (FLACSO-Florida Assets Survey)
ECB	European Central Bank
FLACSO	Facultad Latinoamericana de Ciencias Sociales (Latin American Faculty of Social Sciences)
GDP	Gross Domestic Product
HAB	Habitat (referencing a structure in the film *The Martian*)
IESS	Instituto Ecuatoriano de Seguridad Social (Ecuadorian Institute of Social Security)
IMF	International Monetary Fund
INEC	Instituto Nacional de Estadística y Censos (National Institute of Statistics and Censuses)
JNV	Junta Nacional de la Vivienda (National Housing Board)
LAFTA	The Latin American Free Trade Association
MIDUVI	Ministerio de Desarrollo Urbano y Vivienda (Ministry of Urban Development and Housing)
NGOs	Non-Governmental Organizations
PREVI	Proyecto Experimental de Vivienda (Experimental Housing Project)
QE	Quantitative Easing (economic policy)
RFR	Red Financiera Rural (Rural Financial Network, Ecuador)
SBS	Superintendencia de bancos y seguros del Ecuador (Superintendency of Banks and Insurance Companies, Ecuador)
SEPS	Superintendencia de Economía Popular y Solidaria (Superintendency of Popular and Solidarity Economy, Ecuador)
UIDE	Universidad Internacional del Ecuador
UN-HABITAT	United Nations Human Settlements Programme
USAID	United States Agency for International Development
UVC	Unidad de Valor Constante (Constant Value Unit)
VIS	Vivienda de interés social (social housing programs)

List of Figures

List of Tables

The Spazialization of Debt

Antonio di Campli

Abstract Debt is not just a financial instrument—it is an infrastructure of control that permeates space, shaping cities, homes, and the very conditions of life. These reflections expose how debt functions as a mechanism of dispossession, entrenching economic subjugation while masquerading as opportunity. From mortgage markets to microfinance schemes, financial systems systematically extract value from the labor, aspirations, and vulnerabilities of the indebted. Women, in particular, bear the brunt of this financial colonization, their unpaid and underpaid labor turned into collateral for survival. The concept of "debtscapes" captures how urban space itself is produced through cycles of financial speculation and coercion, where homes are not shelters but sites of extraction. Against this backdrop, the chapter calls for a radical rethinking of architecture and urban planning—not as neutral disciplines, but as terrains of struggle where spatial justice must be reclaimed from the grip of financialized capitalism.

Keywords Debt spaces · Financialized urbanism · Social Reproduction and debt · Debtscapes of resistance

1 The Assault of the Present on the Rest of Time

1.1 What Does Debt Look like?

If indebtedness is something more than a mental state or juridical condition, and necessarily includes social and political relations as well as specific productivity dynamics, we should be able to find traces of it everywhere, in the spaces and landscapes of dwelling (Atwood 2008). And yet, indebtedness never appears as such.

A. di Campli (✉)
DIST, Interuniversity Department of Urban and Regional Studies and Planning, Politecnico di Torino, Torino, Torino, Italy
e-mail: antonio.dicampli@polito.it

A. di Campli (ed.), *Inhabiting Debt*, The Latin American Studies Book Series,
https://doi.org/10.1007/978-3-031-99886-7_1

There's always a little something that's hidden. It's as if places, and the people who live in them, could always be judged based on their debts and, somehow, appear as if they didn't have any. It's difficult to see the indebtedness working in space, because through it we see a world in which nothing seems to truly belong to itself.

To reflect on the relationship between indebtedness and space we can usefully cite an old essay by Deleuze (1990), *Post-scriptum sur les societies de contrôle*. In this well-known book (one of his last), Deleuze shifts from the "disciplinary societies" analyzed by Foucault toward what he calls "societies of control." Disciplinary societies were defined by confinement structures, for example prisons, hospitals, factories, schools, and family. These institutions redefined individuals as members of the social force: the docile bodies of labor, the patient bodies of the health system, the developing bodies of the education system, the oedipal bodies of the family, etc. Foucault's goal was to understand the entire program of modernity by examining these structures which, in turn, had replaced and rationalized the operations of a previous model of power that he called "sovereign society." Each of these models (sovereign, disciplinary, control) has its "machines," its forms of spatial and temporal organization. The machine of sovereign society was the state machinery centered in the body of the king, invested with natural rights; disciplinary society has the *Panopticon*, the extension of the logic of prisons from the penal system to all the institutions of social conditioning and confinement. However, what are the determinantal machines, decisive places, and prevalent logics of societies of control? This is where Deleuze moves beyond Foucault and outlines a series of objections: where discipline shapes, control modulates; where discipline concentrates and encloses, control dissipates and liquefies; while discipline uses bureaucratic protocols, numbers, and personal signatures to define an individual's identity and relations, the logic of control uses *pin* codes, digital footprints, and retinal and facial scans. We could say that the configuration techniques characterizing disciplinary societies have been reconfigured into the "instantaneous communication" and "continuous monitoring" of societies of control. When we begin to analyze our everyday experiences, we discover elements of continuity and superimposition between these two regimes; nevertheless, what is so distinctively new about societies of control? Undoubtedly the diffusion of different technologies—information technology, telecommunications, and various kinds of digital cultures. In fact, Deleuze cites all these elements, but he adds something unexpected: *l'homme n'est plus l'homme enfermé, mais l'homme endetté*. Man is no longer a man confined, but a man in debt (Deleuze 1990, p. 246).

Deleuze considers that "confinement" and "indebtedness" correspond to two great regimes of power merging specific types of authorities, marked by imperatives, imageries, and separate economic logics. Today we can say that indebtedness had integrated and surpassed confinement and has become the dominant control device. So, what are the characteristics of the current regime of indebtedness?

We know what confinement looks like spatially. For example, *enclosures*, i.e., the "fencing in" policies of state-owned lands, or the *commons* in the English countryside which, beginning in the sixteenth century, were the model used to configure the topography of capitalist agricultural production on a global scale. *Enclosures* triggered processes of country-to-city migration, facilitating the rise of industrial economies and the conception and experimentation of spatial regulation regimes. Confinement has more to do with hedges, ownership deeds, the establishment of *zoning* devices, and with boundaries and jurisdictional mechanisms used to achieve the homogeneity and control of production regimes as well as spaces of dwelling.

The presence of these "machines" is still very visible and it's clear that they will be operating for a long time. Nevertheless, the forms and functions of confinement should be reviewed in light of the crisis of the political models and economic processes to which they are linked. School classrooms, assembly lines, central headquarters, office neighborhoods, city boundaries, the family, permanent contracts, and disciplined tourists: all these places and entities, whose consistency depended on being internally ordered, are now dispersed or dismembered, and externally reconfigured.

Architecture has always provided the best spatial traditions of the regimes of power, from the *Panopticon*, *Central Park*, and *Crystal Palace*, to the diverse modernist and contemporary models of dwelling. It is time we asked ourselves whether or not these confinement structures have reached their limit, beyond which they are unable to expand. The spaces that have been built based on this model will undoubtedly continue to function by themselves, more or less according to the old way of doing things. But when a model can no longer expand in space, the reason behind this inability is the advent of a new dynamics of socio-spatial relations. The current regime of indebtedness is, on the one hand, a resumption of the previous one and, on the other, its radical re-orientation. But how does this turn into space? How can it become visible? We are used to thinking about debt as a pure relation, as something invisible, and even spiritual. Isn't the promise to pay, or the promise to believe, perhaps something that is all the more effective, the more it is based on invisible signs and supports?

The two, big, abstract machines that define our age—the market and the media—are two faces of the same inscriptive-design process, of the same tension toward organizing temporality, marked by a constant process of elaboration and removal of an everlasting debt. In the words of the German director Kluge et al. (1990) it is *der Angriff der Gegenwart auf die übrige Zeit*, the assault of the present on the rest of time. Financialized capitalism literally "consumes" forecasts, plans, or visions in its process of coordinating the present, rather than prefiguring futures capable of steering collective actions. While the oscillation between future present and present future was a distinctive characteristic of the modern concepts of contingency, freedom and choice, these two temporal modes now appear to have collapsed into contemporary financial dynamics (Walter and Wansleben 2019). In these process, the political and economic assessments of possible futures do not sculpt collective pathways toward those futures, and much less foster any form of social learning; instead they are calculatedly assimilated in order to improve coordination between current financial dynamics. They act merely as signs fueling a feverish pursuit for short-term profits in a game between the market and the media that goes in two directions, from the top and bottom (Luhmann 1976). If, on the one hand, every semblance of value aspires to rise from its immediate context, on the other, the vague "elsewhere" of global markets cannot but come to earth in a form of an incessant remodeling of the spaces of dwelling.

This dynamics was perceived by Deleuze who, immediately after indicating the position of indebtedness in our contemporary age, stated that: *Il est vrai que le capitalisme a gardé pour constante l'extrême misère des trois quarts de l'humanité, trop pauvres pour la dette, trop nombreux pour l'enfermement: le contrôle n'aura pas seulement à affronter les dissipations de frontières, mais les explosions de bidonvilles ou de ghettos* (Deleuze 1990, p. 246).[1]

Indebtedness acts as a machine to absorb live labor and drain creative anticipation, drawing on everything that men have in common: the "uncaptured" past, not yet considered as value, and the renewal that is possible in the future. Everything that makes it possible to recognize and realize this broadening of time, everything that rushes vaguely forward or remains a little behind, can show us how to exit the circuits and cycles of debt. It is only in the experience of indebtedness that we can tackle the need to free ourselves of debt and, at the same time, desire to build different ties and spaces of resistance.

2 McNamara's Discourse

It is increasingly difficult to ignore debt in the field of the disciplines of design and urban studies. It has always been a key element in studies on the circulation of capital, the reproduction of capitalism and, in particular, the characteristics of financial systems. Private enterprises depend increasingly on financial markets. This is also true for public policies, ever more influenced by national debt dynamics. Families are also increasingly trapped in vicious cycles of debt to compensate the growing weakness of income from employment and the crisis of social protection mechanisms—a crisis that is beginning to emerge in many areas, be it in the West or the so-called Global South. In particular, the crisis of the Fordism paradigm and the advent of the current economic-political phase based on the dynamics of financial markets has meant that poverty—considered as a condition in which individuals and collectives have a limited or no access to basic goods and services—has become the object of specific policies focusing on the diffusion of private debt, used as a tool to finance poverty (Fama 2017).[2] At the same time, in order to reduce national public

[1]In English: "*It is true that capitalism has retained as a constant the extreme poverty of three quarters of humanity, too poor for debt, too numerous for confinement; control will not only have to deal with erosions of frontiers, but with the explosion within shanty towns or ghettoes.*" The endlessness and intensity of debt will, therefore, be revealed as a partial and incomplete construction.

[2]According to Ho (2015, p. 171), finance can be defined as a "constellation of priorities, practices and ideologies that, in the context of a market economy, are mobilised to search for and convert already existing assets into income streams, investments, or immediate profits". In this respect, the concept of financialization indicates a process to bestow value on material and immaterial objects

debts, austerity has become a buzzword, i.e., government policies and measures often considered as one of the reasons behind the increase in poverty and the promotion of personal microdebts. The two forms of debt are thus interconnected. Policies to reduce public debt fuel poverty; the reaction to this is the diffusion of private debt.

The need to redirect the strategies used to combat poverty was triggered by the "fiasco" of large-scale development plans, chiefly launched in non-Western countries during the period of decolonization linked to the crisis of the Fordist and Keynesian economic-political models. Robert McNamara was the President of the World Bank from 1968 to 1981; in his speech delivered in Nairobi on 24 September 1973 he stated that economic growth policies had to be coupled with measures to combat so-called "absolute" poverty; he specified that this could be achieved by adopting specific measures (McNamara 1969). McNamara's objective was to neutralize the explosion of possible socialist revolutions, especially in countries undergoing decolonization (World Bank 2021). His speech marked a shift toward a new age of economic policies promised by the World Bank; in fact its activities slowly began to support the construction of infrastructures for industrial production and, for example, projects in support of family agriculture, social housing, and health services. However, this shift in direction was part of a manipulative discourse which, instead of addressing the structural causes of poverty, preferred to draw attention to the life of the poor, considered as individuals to be re-educated and inserted in broader economic dynamics, rather than assisted. Individuals to be seduced and, at the same time, made to feel guilty. McNamara spoke frankly about the subjectivity and life of the poor using a discursive technique with which he tried to act within the boundary of an openly biopolitical plan. By expunging the words exploitation and subservience from his speech, the diffusion of financial packages for the economically more fragile, especially women (previously excluded from credit apartheid) led to a specific philosophy about poverty and the poor in particular; they were redefined as active individuals, affected by their own marginal condition and possible "redemption."

Ananya (2010), in particular, has studied these issues; she has focused on the concept of *poverty capital*, a term the Indian scholar uses to indicate situations in which poverty, in specific social and political areas, becomes a resource or economic opportunity for certain actors. According to Roy, the conversion of poverty into capital is chiefly achieved through so-called microcredit, a sort of small sum financing usually granted to subjects who cannot access traditional bank services, thereby creating new economic subjects and, as a result, new terrains of investment. Roy believes that the rhetoric underlying microfinance—linked to the granting of microcredits to poor individuals, chiefly women, i.e., people who do not have the guarantees required by the formal banking system—is an expression of so-called "neoliberal populism." A combination of ideas, policies, and imaginaries intended for fragile subjects and aimed at mobilizing emotionally-charged ideals like

such as physical spaces, relationships, education, imaginaries, in order to generate capital, and produce social, racial, or gender inequalities (Bear et al. 2015).

economic freedom, self-reliance, emancipation, and entrepreneurship in order to promote the expansion of financial markets.[3] However, it is not only the actors of debt, but also the territories, spaces, and living conditions produced by debt that have been mushrooming in the last few decades. Debt has gradually taken on an increasingly important but also opaque social and political role in the processes of spatial production and dwelling practices.[4] In particular, the relationship between financialization and urban development has become a key issues in the public discourse on the city (Arrighi and Silver 2001), especially after the 2008 financial crisis, symbolized by the bankruptcy of the Lehman Brothers, and the crash in the sector of subprime mortgages in the United States. This shock triggered an increase in the role and power of finance in socio-spatial changes, both in urban and rural areas (Rutland 2010; Fields and Uffer 2013; Christophers 2015; Derudder and Taylor 2020; Weber 2010). Debt can be considered not only as an economic relationship, but also as a dwelling practice influenced by desires, anxiety, conflicts, and relationships between debtors and creditors; the latter are considered as subjects with unequal resources, rather than actors engaged in atomized, a-spatial transactions. This practice is implemented using several strategies and forms of spatial production.

Numerous studies are currently tackling the problem of debt, especially in the field of economics and social and political studies.[5] However, in the field of urban studies and design disciplines, the questions we should ask are: how do we live in and produce space, in and through debt? What are its effects in the configuration of domestic space and in the processes of spatial production on an architectural scale and the broader scale of proximity? More in general, can a review of the relationship between debt and space help draft a counter-project of co-existence between different ecologies, economies, desires, and imaginaries, i.e., the outcome of the proliferation of social, ecological, and spatial crises that have followed on from one another for decades?

---

[3] *Poverty capital* acts in various forms; there are industries and organizations that prosper thanks to the perpetuation of poverty. For example, companies that make a profit by selling products or services to economically disadvantaged subjects. Their actions, combined with public policies, are intended to curry consensus or support. In some cases, poverty can be viewed as an opportunity for financial investors who benefit from the precarious economic conditions that exist in certain communities or regions. Finally, some humanitarian organizations or institutions may depend on the presence of poverty to justify their existence. Bersani (2017, p. 9) maintains that the objective of economic policies implemented by big global economic-financial operators is not "the reduction or elimination of debt, but the continuous extraction of value and the perpetuation of the relationship of subservience of the debtors towards the creditors." This means that debt cannot disappear, at most it can change: from public debt as the engine behind capitalistic accumulation during the Fordist period, to private debt as a financial enhancement tool in contemporary bio-cognitive capitalism.

[4] Studies on these issues focus on three main topics: financialization of residential housing (Aalbers 2016, 2017); the role of digital platforms (Schwarz 2017; Shaw 2020); and the pervasiveness of financialization processes (Alami and Dixon 2020; Alami 2023; Eagleton-Pierce 2023).

[5] In particular, regarding "debt capitalism" and the political role played by debt in the dependence of states on markets, see the studies by Perulli (2020).

Debt is the concept which, more than any other, is impermeable to spatial analysis. There are many political, historical, and even semantic reasons behind this resistance to identifying the relationships between debt and spatial production. On the one hand, differences in the contexts, the economy, and the disciplines of design and, on the other, the case-by-case interpretation of the two terms that has made the establishment of a relationship between the concept of debt and that of space impracticable. Apart from this thematic and lexical difficulty, there is another, more basic difficulty which is, in fact, the origin and reason for this difficulty: our "inherence" in the phenomenon we wish to study. The underlying obstacle to understanding the field produced by the interaction between the two terms lies in the fact that we are already "inside" it. This is why the link between the two concepts proves ungraspable. Not because its entry door is blocked, but because we have crossed that threshold a long time ago, before it closed behind us, preventing us from leaving. This is why it is impossible to establish the necessary distance between us and the issue—something that would allow us to analyze and critique it. This happens when one is inside a room and becomes confused with its elements, or when we look too closely at an object, and therefore cannot see its edges. To understand its meaning we must activate an inward-looking approach. But we are prevented from doing this by being too close, and this closeness crushes us against its internal walls.[6]

2.1 *The Spatial Politics of Debt*

Debt, considered as a form of social-economic relationship, has a reach that exceeds even monetary economics and is summarized in a moral imperative that functions as a moral principle and action; the latter now occupies a new centrality in neoliberal policies, especially in the global restructuring processes of power relationships that began in the second half of the 1970s (Stimilli 2015; Avallone 2018).

On the one hand, Harvey (1982) maintains that debt has been used by big industrial and financial groups as a tool to weaken the power acquired by male and female workers at the end of World War II, especially in the West. On the other, debt has been used by institutions like the World Bank and the International Monetary Fund as an instrument that can help counter anti-imperialistic uprisings, especially in countries in the Global South where decolonization was underway. The first structural adjustment programs, launched between the late 1970s and late 1980s, prompted southern countries to adhere to the new debt regime; this had multiple consequences, including the liberalization of local financial sectors, the privatization of basic services (e.g., water), and the reinforcement of extractive economies linked to the export of raw materials (Moore 2015). More recently, on a global scale, the 2007–2008 financial crisis has had a significant impact on levels of public or

[6] Debt is a moral, social, and economic concept defining moral relationships, human relationships, conditions of freedom and subservience. There is extensive literature on this subject; see Graeber (2011); Esposito (2013) and Stimilli (2015).

private indebtedness, especially due to the fact that governments had to implement rescue packages or bailouts for financial institutions in difficulty. This led to an increase in public expenditure and, as a result, an increase in public debt. The crisis also affected the private sector. Families lost part of their wealth due to the collapse of the real estate market and reduction in the value of their investments.[7] These policies helped bailout many institutions but, socially speaking, the processes that led to the impoverishment of part of the population were not tackled successfully; this was reflected by a surge in people resorting to debt. Indeed, the objective of these policies was not to eliminate debt, but to continually lower its value, so that debtors would always be in a position of subservience (Bersani 2017). The so-called "debt trap" continues to be supported by current policies, thus reinforcing fake capital and the diffusion of credit systems; the latter are linked to the use of austerity policies based, among other things, on the containment of wages and income from employment which is therefore increasingly vulnerable to consumption indebtedness (Harvey 2011).[8] According to David Harvey (2017), this situation is managed by central banks that tend to print more money through *quantitative easing*, indirectly supporting processes of real estate speculation.[9] This measure has led to an unsustainable increase in house prices in nearly all major cities in the world. It reveals one of the links between debt policies and the housing crisis. In the end, what David Harvey had foreseen actually took place, i.e., the gap between workers' earnings and their spending capacity has been filled by the advent of credit cards and an increase in debt (2011, p. 29). The overall result is that a large part of the population is engaged either in looking for money to pay debts or a job with a pay check so that they can ask for a loan, and thus resume the debt merry-go-round.

In the last few decades, one of the main objectives of financial policies has been financial inclusion and greater access to credit by those who were traditionally excluded from the formal financial services markets in many countries, and in Latin

[7] Financial institutions and banks had, in particular, overexploited so-called financial leverage, borrowing enormous amounts of money to invest in risky assets such as subprime *mortgages*, thus increasing the effects of risky housing loans. Financial institutions created complex tools, such as collateralized securities from mortgage loans and debt guaranteed by securities; this has made it difficult to assess the true value and risk of these investments. When the real estate market and *subprime mortgages* began to collapse, these institutions found themselves burdened with huge losses and were very vulnerable to risk; this triggered a global financial crisis.

[8] The other face of debt, however, is usually kept hidden, because the debate about the crisis of ordinary debt merges two completely different processes: on the one hand, the credit system; on the other, living in debt. Many analyses regarding debt and the financial crisis concentrate on the first process (Denning 2011).

[9] *Quantitative easing* (QE) tends to reduce long-term interest rates. Lower rates make mortgage loans and other construction loan agreements more accessible and convenient. This encourages the demand for housing and other property assets, leading to price hikes. At the same time, due to the low yields of more traditional investments such as government bonds, investors try to find higher yields by investing in more risky assets, such as the real estate market. This fuels property speculation, with investors who try to make a profit from the increase in house prices. Finally, QE can help relaunch the economy by increasing the trust of consumers and investors. When the economy gets stronger, the demand for housing could increase, pushing up prices.

America in particular.[10] If, on the one hand, the increase in the number of microfinance institutions in the region has undoubtedly increased access to credit (Peck and Miller 2006; De la Torre et al. 2011), on the other, the recent microcredit crises in Latin America and other so-called "developing" countries have triggered concern regarding the excessive indebtedness among the more vulnerable classes caused by the expansion of microfinance (Schicks 2013a; Bastiaensen et al. 2013). Figueroa (2011) believes that so long as wealth inequality in Latin America remains high, the region will continue to be characterized by a three-tier financial structure: private banks, formal non-banking institutions (e.g., savings and loan cooperatives), and the informal sector (primarily moneylenders, but also family and friends). Given this situation, economically weaker subjects pay more to access formal credit compared to their stronger counterparts. This wealth inequality produces market segmentation; rich people turn to banks, the less rich to formal non-banking institutions, and the poor to the informal sector.[11]

One theory proposed by several people is that we are structurally becoming a society of people in debt, not only in the south of the world, but also in the West (Graeber 2011; Lazzarato 2012). This is because debt servitude not only remains the main method used to hire low-cost labor in many parts of the world, but also because most salaried employees in western countries often work to repay mortgages, loans with interest, and in some cases moneylenders. The very biopolitical nature of this activity should not be ignored by those involved in urban studies. Examples include the situation endured by migrants who have to work, almost without pay, for the criminals who manage the labor market in big rural extractive territories (Gudynas 2009; Acosta 2016; Mezzadra and Neilson 2019), or graduates who, especially in the United States, spend years repaying the loans they took to pay university fees or health treatments (Kluender et al. 2021).[12] The outcome of the

[10] Credit is a method used to loan financial resources to an institution or individual and expect to receive a return in the future. A loan is money or an asset given to someone for a period of time accompanied by the promise by the receiver to return it, usually with interest. Debt normally refers to one or more obligations or liabilities pursuant either to a loan of money or acquisition of assets and services based on credit. In normal parlance, loans and debts are often interchangeable terms.

[11] A distinctive trait of this financial structure is that credit costs more if it is granted by non-bank institutions compared to formal banks. Likewise, the credit granted by the informal sector is more expensive to repay compared to the credit obtained from formal non-bank institutions. This is primarily due to the role of the guarantees that can be provided by the indebted subjects to reduce risk and also to the economies of scale in the transaction costs for big loans (Floro and Messier 2006).

[12] Austerity policies imposed by foreign debt, above all in the West, together with inflation and the ensuing loss of purchasing power by wages, has made debt necessary in order to access essential goods such as food and medicines. Impoverishment has accelerated indebtedness to cope with everyday needs and pay services such as water, gas, and electricity. Debt as a financial technology has become widespread as a means to deal with precariousness. The unique feature of this phenomenon is that indebtedness is no longer associated with the occasional consumption of an asset or service, but has become a permanent obligatory way to integrate a gradually decreasing income. It involves what some social scholars, especially in Latin America, call superdebt or the "financial colonisation of social reproduction" (Federici et al. 2021), in other words the entry of finance into key sectors of social reproduction, e.g., food, health, education, medical assistance, and housing.

balance of power between unequal players is created, and continuously reactivated, by the "neoliberal machine," by the establishment of its platforms and logistics networks (Springer 2016). But there's a difference. In societies with generalized debt, it's as if the destiny of being subservient (once reserved to the south of the world) has now spread and involves everyone. While in our modern age the strong part of the world should welcome the weak part within its boundaries, today the weak part appears to have sucked the strong part back into its own void (of economic resources). For example, the way major banks in the United States treat their creditors is currently similar to the way the World Bank treated indebted countries: the conditions imposed on the sale of mortgages to impoverished families inevitably leads to insolvency. The sale of these mortgages gambles on how long it will take the holder to go broke. This means inserting "mortgage" and "gamble" in a single product and reselling it to institutional investors (which are perhaps the pension funds of the mortgage holder), maintaining that it will undoubtedly pay off in any event, thereby allowing the investors to let these packages circulate as if they were cash. The strategy is to flip the responsibility of settling the gamble onto a huge insurance group which, if it succumbs under the weight of the debt (which actually occurs), then it will be rescued by the money of the contributors. In other words, all this looks like an unusually elaborate version of the way in which banks lent money to the dictators in Bolivia and Gabon in the late 1970s: they granted irresponsible loans, knowing full well that, if insolvency occurred, politicians and bureaucrats would act to ensure that the creditors be reimbursed one way or another, notwithstanding the number of human lives that would have to be devastated to achieve that goal (Devlin and French-Davis 1995). In some respects, we are witnessing a domestic percolation of public debt or a hybridization between private and public debt. Just think of the migrants who get into debt to cross the Mediterranean, or the many female microcredit policies launched in countries like India, Nepal or Mexico; the aim is to trigger basic productive economies. In these extreme cases, the debt is linked to "naked survival."[13] However, a more frequent occurrence is that the debt is something that insinuates itself opaquely in life projects, imaginaries and relationships between economies (Zapata 2013; Harker 2017; Datta and Aznar 2019).

3 Debt Is Space

The theory proposed here is that debt is not only an economic and temporal issue, but a real "dwelling practice" that occurs based on precise forms of spatial production. Space that is produced within the framework of obligatory conditions, interwoven combinations of forms of predation and extractive production, failures, and strategies of resistance, ruin, and rupture. So, as architects and urban planners, how

[13] The term "bare survival" refers to a condition in which human life is reduced to a biological state, without its political, social, or cultural dimensions.

do we tackle these dynamics? How do we deal with the fact we are involved with bodies and spaces produced in these obligatory conditions? What view should we take of "lives in debt" as described by Harney and Moten (2013)?

Debt is a state in which a person owes money. A promise. This kind of commitment is traditionally considered to be a temporal and social relationship. In his book entitled *Debt: The First 5000 Years* (2011), David Graeber emphasizes the social dimension, as does Lazzarato (2015, p. 70) who states that time and duration are key elements in debt. Not only work time and life time, but also time as a possibility, as future. Peebles (2010) indicates the ability to link the present to the future as a fundamental characteristic of debt. This idea of debt is exemplified in the IMF's definition of debt as outstanding financial liabilities from past loans (IMF 2017). Ordinarily, debt is the action of borrowing in the present and reimbursing in the future (Mauss 1954; Bourdieu 1977; Derrida 1992). However, debt is not simply an economic tool; it is also and above all a technique to govern and control individual and collective subjectivities, i.e., it is a political construct. A mix of ideas, imaginaries, needs, and fears. However, it is crucial we consider debt as a spatial as well as temporal relationship if we wish to understand the way indebtedness is experienced and its social and spatial effects.

Debt is, above all, a biopolitical fact. It is pedagogical and punitive; it combines politics and policy. Debt is one of the few places where microeconomics and macroeconomics are intricately intertwined; for example, personal debt increases just like public debt tends to increase. Debt is sometimes a story about giving, and sometimes about taking. It is always a story about extractive capitalism, i.e., a relationship individualized with a similarly naturalized economy, almost always based on exploitation. So, given that a promise of property ownership and a desire to produce space is also expressed by this system of relationships and constraints, the question is: can debt become a principle behind the elaboration of spatial analysis? Can the debt machine become a design tool in the same way, for example, that contemporary ecological, health, and climatic crises have redefined the topics and forms of design action?

As mentioned earlier, debt is an "interior" with difficult-to-identify contours. In order to exit something that does not have an exterior, we need to reflect on how we interpret those contours and on the conceptual languages we have inherited from an age-old tradition, rather than on the traits of socio-economic processes and their interlinked spatial ecologies. We should engage in a conversion of the significance of the debt regime in which we are embroiled. We must avoid presuming we can free ourselves from this regime by returning to the situation that existed before the current crisis, as if this latter crisis had produced the debt. On the contrary, it is the debt that has contributed to determining the current ecological, climatic, social, and health crisis (Harney and Moten 2013). There is, however, something we can do: instead of trying to stop a now unstoppable dynamic, we can try to distort it, turning this chain of obligations into circuits of resistance and solidarity. There are two ways to do this: either by turning insolvency into an option of freedom rather than a declaration of servitude, or by trying to socialize the debt, reinterpreting it in terms of design, and trying to develop a philosophy regarding the configuration of socially useful spaces and goods. In this case, debt will not disappear but change, shedding the traditional notion of "development" and "production" and shifting toward Latour's (2020) idea of "generation" and "dependence." The difference between an analysis of the forms of dwelling and spatial production considered in terms of productive systems, and an analysis based on generative processes is, firstly, the principle behind them: freedom for the former, dependence for the latter. Secondly, due to the role assigned to man, absolutely central for the former, dissipated for the latter; finally, they differ as regards their type of movement, mechanical for the former, generating for the latter. The production system is based on a certain concept of nature, materialism, and the role of science. It is based on the division between human actors and their resources. The basic idea behind this is that the freedom of the subjects is deployed in a natural framework in which it is possible to acknowledge precise limits for each property. The generative system involves agents, actors, and living beings with separate reactivities. It is not based on the same concept of materiality, does not have the same epistemology, and does not lead to the same policies. It is not interested in producing for mankind based on resources, but on generating ecologies without accumulations or specializations. Generation does not pursue a project of emancipation, but is based on dynamics of dependency. To depend means, first and foremost, to limit. It does not involve living in harmony with natural agents. We must avoid the obstacle of believing that it is possible to live empathically with everyone. The objective is not to try to be in agreement with all the agents, but learnt to depend on them.[14] To achieve this goal we need to counter, in particular, the orthodox economic concept of debt; the latter explains its current proliferation also in the West thanks to the neoliberal language of financial inclusion, free choice, and individual responsibility (Foucault 2008; Povinelli 2011).[15]

Social, economic, and political literature provide a starting point from which to embark on a spatial reflection on debt. In particular, Peebles (2010) emphasizes how at least four spatial elements interact in the notion of debt: mobility, place, distribution, and boundaries. However, in these studies space is chiefly considered as a smooth surface, as a passive element. Nevertheless, debts plays a key role in the creation of pathways and transnational networks, for example the ones linked to remittances, to the international development programs linking financial markets to the suburbs of the middle classes (Mauss 1954), and also regional city-countryside relationships. We can state that debt models the movement of bodies in space, on different levels.

The studies by Christopher Harker (2014) focus on the processes of indebtedness in Palestinian communities in Ramallah; drawing on these studies, the first level of discussion about debt as a spatial phenomenon is to consider it as a typology. The topology concentrates on the qualitative properties of space (as against its geometric properties). Typologically speaking, a space is not the distance between its points

[14] Regarding the concept of dependency as a spatial category and design option, see the book by di Campli and Gabbianelli (2022), *Delinking. Lo spazio della coesistenza*, in particular the chapter *Dichiarazione di dipendenza*.

[15] See also Gago and Cavallero (2019) regarding microcredits in Argentina.

when it is in a fixed state, but rather the characteristics that maintain the process of distortion and transformation (flexion, stretch, and compression). Topology is a special kind of relational space in which the gap between "here" and "there" is not measured in meters or kilometers, but in social relations, exchanges, and interactions. Harker maintains that the typologies of debt are produced by "spatial acts," for example by turning to a bank or relatives and friends. These spatial relationships, that connect indebted subjects to figures and institutions that lend them money, are invisible strings that can stretch and ramify. At any given moment, and in any given place, there are bank loans that prevail in a certain context, but family debt, for example, especially informal debt not negotiated with legal institutions such as banks, is often the result of processes that occur on several levels, from local to transnational; it is here that relationships with relatives or one's clan come into play. In this multiscalar and opaque dimension of the relationship between debt and space, money flows link parts of cities or entire neighborhoods to big metropolitan centers and rural contexts.[16] These tendrils (more or less interwoven relational networks) "turn" into physical spaces, into structures of dwelling, into urban layouts, in some cases, into infrastructure systems. These processes reflect the spatial possibilities of debt, creating "demand for debt"; they themselves are places in which debt typologies are constantly recreated. This second level of analysis of the relationship between debt and space, focusing on the identification and analysis of intertwined ties between economies, times, subjects and forms of dwelling, is one way to think about debt considered as "spatial ecology," rather than as a simple temporal relationship.

In the West, debt has also become a key means with which to live a "modern" life, to obtain increasingly better levels of comfort and protection in a context in which the notion of the future has, for some time now, been in crisis. In Italy, in particular, social pressure to consume and maintain a socio-economic status, exasperated by a diffuse desire for approval, is reflected in the growth of the credit market and accommodating policies to access loans granted by banks and financial institutions (Milani 2016; D'Alessio and Iezzi 2016). All this appears to spatially turn into special forms of touristic "consumption" of places that provide intense bodily experiences or into the desire for continuous technological upgrading of one's life spaces and structures.

To spatially discuss these ecologies of debt, we can usefully discriminate between public debt and private debt.

Public debt, especially foreign debt, is considered to be one of the causes for the incredible expansion of slums in countries of the Global South (Davis 2006).[17] As

---

[16] Like many subjects who decide to move from the country to the city and become indebted often to relatives and informal moneylenders, debt geographies are marked by obligations and power logics which, in some cases, are the expression of forms of violence (Berlant 2011) and the persistent condition of social and economic distress that is "crude, corrosive and bereft of events" (Povinelli 2011, p. 145).

[17] Most narratives about the diffusion of debt in slums focus on the role and possibility for families and indebted subjects to be seen as victims, heroes, or *tricksters* (UN-HABITAT 2003a, b).

noted by Sell and Kunitz (1986), indebtedness ensures participation, albeit peripheral, in the world's economy, and increased involvement of external actors in a country's internal social and economic affairs. In the last 30 years, external actors have had an unprecedented influence in shaping the macroeconomic context of many countries in the global south thanks to the extension of credit and the ensuing diffuse crisis regarding the fulfilment of debt service obligations.

External debt indirectly influences the expansion of slums by implementing several dynamics. In the first place, excessive debt inputs into social and economic restructuring, driving rural migrants toward urban areas that are often not able to satisfy the growing demand for employment and infrastructure (Davis 2006; UN-HABITAT 2003b). This dependent urbanization, shaped by exogenous pressure, is a factor that enhances the growth of slums. Foreign debt also contributes to rapid urbanization, promoting extractive economies linked to agriculture and the export of raw materials; the aim is to obtain foreign currency in order to repay the debt. In turn, agricultural production for exportation is generally characterized by processes of environmental simplification, increasing mechanization, and a consequent reduction in employment. Secondly, debt facilitates a substantial outflow of capital, thus limiting productive investments in the national economy. Payments of public debt services involve reducing state investments to improve public services, thus contributing to currency devaluation and a reduction in the purchasing power of consumers, within a context of rapid urbanization (Ferraro and Rosser 1994; UN-HABITAT 2003b).

4 The Domestic in Conflict

The expression *Buy land, they aren't making it anymore* is said to have been pronounced by Mark Twain.[18] Perhaps the North American writer wasn't entirely right. Land is not the real object of transactions. The scarcity of land is only one of the conditions defining market conditions, because what is really for sale is not the land or the buildings, but the means with which to access them; in other words, debt. So in many ways the real estate market is a place where debt is bought and sold, a place where the house is ultimately only a medium. However, market conditions are not the same for everyone. While the rich can obtain money at relatively low rates and the middle class at slighter higher rates, the poor can only obtain money at very high rates. This system has to be continuously fueled by two-way debt. At the top, builders obtain financing through debt to buy land and fight against the regulations of the system to plan and build houses (at great risk). At the bottom, citizens take out increasingly costly mortgages so they can buy real estate (at great risk). When prices soar, mortgages increase, and so do prices. And risks. Loans can be considered as mortgage-backed securities; although they can be exchanged, in the end the entire

[18] *The Ladies' Home Journal*, 1979, n. 96, p. 10.

system can break down; it is ironic that when this happens governments have to borrow even more to try and keep the system going. Much water has passed under the bridge since the 2008 crisis, but this principle still governs the production of most of our dwelling spaces.

In brief we can say that producing a habitat through debt spatially involves five main domains. The first is the construction of housing units and settlements directly linked to the sale of mortgages. The inhabitants are "virtual" owners because the banks hold the ownership deeds for the duration of the mortgage; this involves a commitment to make monthly payments. The second field of action involves the purchase of already consolidated urban spaces, inhabited by the working class, where it is possible to launch urban enhancement and regeneration policies linked to the trigger of gentrification and ensuing eviction of economically vulnerable individuals and families. The third domain involves the financial colonization processes of informal and working-class habitats, primarily thanks to so-called micro-financial practices.[19] According to Raquel Rolnik (2018), informal settlements in particular are spaces where financial colonization is easier to implement, i.e., spaces subject to predatory financial practices due to the lack of regulations and support by public institutions. The fourth field of action is visible primarily in Latin American or African countries; it is produced when infrastructures (e.g., mobility infrastructures) are implemented by the State or private entities in territories that are considered empty; this triggers spontaneous urbanization, nearly always linked to informal debt processes. The last domain coincides with migration processes and spaces. Debt can move a human body from one place to another, rooting it in its point of arrival in a doubly confined condition, not only from the point of view of space, but also its economic ties. In all the aforementioned cases, debt spatially acts on several levels, mixing scales that range from the transnational to the local. However, what appears to be noteworthy in the field of design and urban studies are the ways in which debt reshapes the relationships between the domestic and urban dimension.

Gago and Cavallero (2022) maintain that houses have currently become a laboratory and space of colonization. What does this mean? How is this change in the domestic dimension reflected on the urban or proximity scale? Finally, how is indebtedness reflected in the demands for and policies of dwelling?

Judith Butler has written that revolution sometimes occurs when no one wants to go home (2011). What does this statement indicate today when the meaning of domestic condition is changing? What happens when the home is besieged by debts and violence?

The late twentieth century witnessed a series of crises in the fields of health, economy, climate, energy, and ecology. During those crises several dynamics became more intense and interconnected. The increased indebtedness of families to

[19] Compared to the sums granted by the traditional financial sector, microfinance is a system of financial products and services involving relatively small sums; it is intended to be used by so-called "non-bankable" individuals or collectives, i.e., excluded from traditional financing due to their socio-economic status. Microfinance uses tools such as micro-credit, micro-insurance, and micro-leasing, paid by migrants.

buy basic necessities due to a reduction in income became embroiled with the reorganization and intensification of forms of reproductive labor, especially unpaid labor, due to the advent of the financial technology (FinTech) used by families as mobile systems of payment, i.e., electronic wallets, online platforms and digital banking.[20]

The house is a space where new forms of financing have "landed"; these forms turn the crisis into a laboratory of experimentation, extracting value and intensifying forms of paid and unpaid labor. It is there—where capital has historically wanted to display a "nonproductive" space—that decisive forms of enhancement currently come together. It is the ensemble of these dynamics that makes it possible to rethink the house, no longer as a private, intimate place, but as a battlefield, not only due to the intrusion of new financial technologies, but also as a place where labor is reorganized.

In the growing divide between needs and income, and in the relationship between habitat and the diffusion of domestic indebtedness, the financial sector acts as an "extractive" operator, literally withdrawing value from the employment sector, above all the female employment sector. In particular, in countries in the Global South it is often the female members of the family who try and produce more income in order to pay the debts incurred to purchase goods and services such as housing, education, or health benefits. They experience indebtedness as a process expropriating not only time, energy, physical and mental resources, but also as a politicizing process. The material construction of the house is possible through debt: brick after brick, ceiling after ceiling, walls, window and door frames, tiles, furniture, and decorations on more or less garish façades; this phenomenon politicizes the terrain of social reproduction, opening the traditionally confined space of the house (its domestic interior) and blurring the boundary between house and neighborhood. The result is the configuration of "domestic territories" characterized by conditions of control, subservience, and resistance.[21]

The fact that social reproductive labor is a politicizing activity is not a novel concept (Meehan and Strauss 2015; Bhattacharya 2017; Federici 2020; Gago 2020; Mitchell et al. 2004). When women produce habitat, they use unique methods to interface with debt. Some consider debt as an opportunity, almost a duty. Being in debt allows them to enhance their homes and increase their livelihood. Being in debt means that they monetize desires and aspirations; female labor is turned into forms of production and reproduction of unequal urban spaces. The incremental processes

[20] Platforms use housing as both a remote workplace and as a place to "store" goods and assets, producing a spatial indistinctness that mixes everything up. The everyday spaces of families are turned into financial "terminals" (attracting the attention of financial instruments of debt, consumption and revenue capture), but are also intensified as value production sites (reproductive labor, telework, and new forms of home-based work) that are exploited by several speculative circuits.

[21] In her analysis of the class dynamics of microfinance, Federici (2019) maintains that debt has mystified class relationships by creating an endless number of entrepreneurs who invest in its reproduction.

required to produce a habitat means that "the construction of the house never ends." Once the first loan is obtained to put certain basic necessities in place, e.g., the plumbing in the bathroom, the floors in the rooms, or the purchase of household appliances, people begin to think of how to enlarge the house to accommodate their children's needs or make a space where they can work, thus densifying and inputting into the growth of neighborhoods with very few services. A times, these neighborhoods are also stigmatized.

The politicization of domestic space is an old flagship demand by feminists. Several studies and essays have revealed that this is where value is produced, where the care to sustain life is both invisible and indispensable. Being shut in the house corresponds to a political order and patriarchal hierarchy systems (Mezzadri 2019; Navarro 2016). In particular, Maria Mies (1986) has examined the relationship between capitalism and domesticity in the field of social studies. Her research could be based on the following question: why does capitalism feel it needs to create a space of isolation and consumption so that women, in particular, are induced by them to seek out privacy and intimacy, and thus consider the house as a "domestic hearth"?[22] Mies maintains that the family space is redefined as a field to create needs; its configuration is based on a hygienist euphoria, a place where the subsumption of reproduction takes place within heteronormative family logics.[23] The domestic dimension is produced in capitalism as a process of interiorization and identification of a space of "confinement." It is above all women who have been confined at home, in a place considered "private," where there is less of a possibility for them to take on leadership roles. The way in which these "domesticated" bodies are exploited primarily requires that their tasks be socially discredited; only then is it possible to justify their confinement and the naturalization of their work, to be exploited without pay.[24]

The economic, social, and ecological crises that follow on from one another have led to the intensification and transformation of the notion of domesticity. In the home, women have to take on more and more tasks; in some cases, they have to live with men who are sometimes violent. The space that has always been considered the chief supporter of life and bodies, appears increasingly characterized by a precariousness which, in theory, it should counter.

[22] According to Mies, in the process of domestication, domestic space becomes an "internal colony" of (European) men while it colonizes "foreign" territories. Colonization and domestication are therefore processes that go hand-in-hand and allow us to interpret the logic of mutual implication characterizing the structure of colonial and patriarchal capitalism.

[23] Mies affirms that domestication involves the externalization of costs which would otherwise be chargeable to capitalists. This means that a woman's work is considered a natural resource, freely available like water and air. This produces an army of hidden workers. As a result, male proletarianization does not exist without the domestication of women's bodies.

[24] In some ways these issues recall the demands by the Domestic Salary Campaign launched in the 1970s, *Campaña por el salario doméstico*, that used the slogan "houses are our factories" (Federici and Austin 2017).

It is vital we understand the productive and reproductive dimension of domestic space.[25]

Incommensurability characterizes reproductive labor, the labor performed by vulnerable, peripheral, or marginal individuals, such as women and people who live in the country. This issue was tackled by Federici (2011) in her book entitled *Calibán y la bruja. Mujeres, cuerpo y acumulación originaria.* She analyzed the traits of capitalism from a female perspective, tapping into Marxist, workerist, feminist, and Foucault-type theories.[26] She theorizes that the affirmation of the capitalist regime not only made domestic labor invisible (including activities such as care of the children and house, and the production of goods to be used by the family), but that there was an intensification of the naturalization of female reproductive labor, presented as if it were a vocation.[27] Other female-oriented reflections on the issue of "disproportionate" domestic labor focused on notions such as "value-affection" and "value-community," in order to prompt people to think about other forms of consideration of value and other productive activities, i.e., beyond an assessment based only on salary (Morini 2010). According to the rationale of capitalism, the female perspective is the most destabilizing perspective, involving the calculation and assessment of value. Unaccounted invisible labor is "disproportionate." This is exactly what is exploited by the financial tools colonizing the house, because microscopic pedagogies take place in the house (Murard and Zylberman 1976) and finally become imaginaries, habits, and architectural spaces which, according to Lazzarato and Alliez (2021), act as machines that make it possible to incessantly produce and reproduce value. Therefore the notion of domestic labor contains a paradox. We talk about labor, but by calling it either domestic or basic labor, it is ostensibly no longer labor. We acknowledge it has value, yet it appears to be fundamentally symbolic and emergency-based. Whatever the case may be, this product is a naturalization of certain tasks, practices and, above all, bodies.

[25] Alessandra Mezzadri makes this comment about the work performed by Maria Mies, "Mies" analysis of home-based work challenges the theorizations that propose strict separation between the realms of production and reproduction; these separations screen the value generated by social reproductive labor (2019, p. 35).

[26] Silvia Federici concentrates on the analysis of the processes of privatization and expropriation of English peasants from their land starting in the eighteenth century, through the creation of *enclosures*, fences that surrounded a piece of land, assigning an owner assets that previously belonged to everyone. A process that was accompanied by the beginning of the colonization of the Americas. We could say, therefore, that there is no internal colonization of debt without external colonization.

[27] In this context, a woman's body in particular has become a crucial condition behind the existence of a labor force. This is due to the fact that when a capitalist turns labor into goods, he subordinates the activity of his workers to an external order, over which they have no control, and with which they cannot identify. This process leads to a dissociation vis-à-vis the body. The body becomes live capital. We can therefore say that the first machine developed by capitalism was the human body and not the steam engine.

5 Debtscapes

Appadurai (1996) calls the urban spaces of debt, *debtscapes*, i.e., urban forms produced by precise political-economic dynamics in order to provide answers to a problem of dwelling.[28] While working-class neighborhoods have always been places of contention, their conceptualization as landscapes of debt refers specifically to the gender policies and practices expressed by the social reproductive labor undertaken by their inhabitants (Aalbers 2016). Working-class neighborhoods redefined as *debtscapes*, especially in places in the Global South, can broadly speaking be interpreted as a domestic territory created by complex social reproductive labor implemented by vulnerable subjects. Especially female subjects. The focus on redefining the domestic features of the house, and the fact that neighborhood urban space becomes domestic, is in some ways an attempt to establish a "feminist interpretation of debt" (Federici et al. 2021), demonstrating how social reproductive labor circulates and passes through bodies, interiors, and parts of cities, triggering an inversion between interior and exterior in dwelling practices. In particular, the emergence of these processes enables a revision of the vitality of popular economies, based primarily on the bodies of women and their work, considered as productive sectors of the financialization and creation of value. We can therefore affirm that debt is a special form of extractivism leading to the production of a "body-territory" (Gago 2020, pp. 84–114) whose spatiality breaks down the traditional "domestic enclosure."[29] In other words, debt challenges the binary relationship between the internal domestic space of the house and that of the neighborhood. Between public and private.

The body is never abstract; it is crossed by, and crosses, different conditions of intensity and transformations, subject to continuous changes in the conditions it inhabits. Veronica Gago (2022, p. 120) states: *The conjunction of the words "body" and "territory" speaks for itself: it says that it is impossible to cut apart and isolate the individual body from the collective body, the human body from the territory and landscape. "Body-territory," compacted as a single word, deliberalises the notion*

[28] In his book *Modernity at Large* (1996), Arjun Appadurai uses versions of the concept of landscape, such as *ethnoscape*, *mediascape*, *technoscape*, *financescape*, and *ideoscape*, to describe the flows of globalized capitalism at the intersection between culture, politics, and the economy. The concept of *debtscape*, in particular, describes how individual and collective debts become a form of control and power, influencing the relationships between individuals, communities, and countries.

[29] This concept, invented to define ecological conflicts and, in particular, the struggle against mining megaprojects in Latin America, places extractivism beyond the defense of indigenous territories and the conflicts of appropriation of raw materials, extending it to the relationship between finance and the production of urban and sub-urban spaces. In particular, within the context of decolonial philosophy, the concept of "body-territory" often assumes a critical and political perspective, referring to the link between the human body and the territory, not only in a physical sense, but also in terms of power, control, and colonial history, highlighting how political and cultural control has been exerted over the individually considered body, but also over the collective territory (Anzaldúa 1987).

of the body as individual property and specifies a political, productive, and epistemological continuity, of the body as territory. The human form emerges not as a solitary entity but as an assemblage of shared capacities, potentials, and intensities that transcend individuality. These elements become distinct only as they are filtered through the lived experience of each person, emphasizing that existence is never isolated—bodies are shaped by collective interactions, human and nonhuman alike. The fusion of *corporeal being* and *spatial belonging* further challenges notions of absence; neither body nor territory can be framed as "missing" or deficient. Instead, this perspective reframes systemic displacement and appropriation, not as voids to be filled, but as processes that demand critical attention to how power and agency are distributed across interconnected systems.

The combination of the colonization of bodies and the diffusion of microfinance practices and formal indebtedness in politically fragile contexts has configured debt landscapes which, according to Gago and Cavallero (2022), contain certain "revolutionary features because they are both places of political dispute and the establishment of strategies to redefine the meaning and value of informal popular economies" (Gago 2017; Simone 2019). According to the two authors, the revolutionary dimension of debt landscapes is linked to the ways in which women, in particular, sustain the way in which microfinance expropriates resources, energies, and time, and also, for example, defines spaces of demand.[30] The empowerment of women encouraged by microfinance sponsored, for example, by so-called micro-loans, is usually associated with the notion of freeing women from oppressive family and social ties, as well as inadequate living conditions.[31] When the individuals reorganize space they gain a certain independence and can enjoy a significant use value of the house; however, what microfinance really puts into value, i.e., that which is extracted and capitalized, is the value produced by the incremental construction of the dwelling, and the value inherent in the social reproductive labor accompanying the search for an independent life.

In this respect, microfinance is expropriating, because it not only facilitates exploitation of the work produced by hard-working bodies, but also expropriates the value that their reproductive labor creates due to the interest rates pocketed by the microfinance institute (Fraser 2014). But debt policy is even more ambivalent. While reflecting on this issue, Jabary-Salamanca (2022) maintains that we need to

[30] Based on reflections by Appadurai (1996) and Ananya (2010) demonstrates how *debtscapes* and *riskscapes* have become a key characteristic of what she calls *bottom billion* capitalism, a term that refers to an economic perspective that draws attention to the roughly billion individuals considered to be the poorest in the world. This idea was put forward by the economist Collins (2008) in his book, *The Bottom Billion*; in it he examines the socio-economic conditions of countries that represent the most impoverished part of the world's population.

[31] The term microloan indicates the granting of small financial loans to low-income individuals or small businesses that cannot access traditional bank services. Microcredit is almost a synonym of microloan. However, the latter emphasizes the concept of loan, suggesting that the money has to be returned within a specific period of time: the former has a much broader meaning, including not only loans in the narrow sense of the word, but other financial services such as savings, insurance, and money transfer.

broaden our knowledge of social reproduction by moving beyond the scale and dimension of the house and consider material infrastructures such as the pipes, sewers, or electricity as part of the domestic sphere. When women from working-class neighborhoods organize to improve the supply of services and develop interactions between multiple entities and subjects, they politicize and extend the domestic realm of the house, questioning the power relations in which they are involved. Small incremental actions—for example, advocating for a child who is not receiving proper education or holding a local government accountable for miserable housing conditions—are experienced as personal frustrations that transform personal emotions and sentiments into politically charged affects (Gökarıksel 2016, p. 226). This process corresponds to a politicization of the debt and becomes policies of visibility. Investments to improve the home, open spaces, or infrastructures in the neighborhood simultaneously highlight insufficient dwelling and urban policies as well as the presence of situations that are about to collapse. Financing the social reproductive work performed by women leads to the construction and politicization of the city; it turns the intimate space of the house into a battlefield that spreads to its surroundings and redefines the neighborhood as a domestic space of protest. By so doing, debt is not only something that expropriates or politicizes, it is also something that makes the boundary between the house, neighborhood and city permeable, as it does the boundary between bodies and spaces.

All this produces special relationships, including process of subservience, desire for emancipation, and economic calculation. As mentioned earlier, indebtedness, especially domestic indebtedness, has increased during the last financial, social, climatic, and health crises. Although in areas in the Global South the processes of household indebtedness are nothing new, several specific conditions have been triggered by the increase in the financialization of urban economies, and in particular urban-rural interface contexts (Deere and Catanzarite 2016; Deere and Contreras 2011), associated with the recurrent economic and political crises that have recently occurred, for example in Latin American countries. On the one hand, there has been an increase in people's desire for emancipation and independence, especially in the collectives and individuals with a rural background who migrate to cities. These ambitions turn into a growing desire for consumption and in a widespread willingness to take on relationship debt. On the other, real wages are either stagnant or decreasing and social protection is traditionally weak in those places. So debt is the answer to the need and desire to make ends meet and improve one's social status, trying to break free of oppressive social constraints and relationships. In many urban areas, especially in Latin America, indebtedness, in particular household indebtedness, tends to be hybrid; it is both formal and informal, created by mixing sources like banks and savings cooperatives with informal lenders or loan sharks (Deere and Catanzarite 2017). This hybridization sparks continuous renegotiations and "transfer" of the debt among multiple sources; it is marked by the friction produced by the desire for independence of the indebted subjects and the persistence of rural-type social practices characterized by orbital relationships and dependence between multiple subjects and places. In countries in the south, especially in Latin

America, debt triggers a redefinition of the relationship between urbanity and rurality, between *ciudad letrada* and *campo* (Rama 1984).[32]

Debt is therefore a structure interweaving desires of emancipation and processes of reinforcement of preexisting relationships of subalternity and inequality in categories such as gender, ethnicity, and social status.

Power and social differentiation shape the processes of indebtedness; this simultaneously produces conditions of dependence and strategies to resist the debt, i.e., the outcome of hybridizations between economies and the configuration of precise spatial set ups and structures. In this respect, the widespread belief about the alleged financial illiteracy of the indebted subjects, especially rural subjects, who live in the suburbs of medium-sized Latin American cities, does not take into account the complexity and subtlety of their budget management and debt strategies. On the one hand, the remarkable ability of the indebted subjects to find multiple, and sometimes astonishing, ways to take control of finance and microfinance tools. These subjects do not passively use credit services, but interpret them based on their own reference framework, adapting them and often circumventing the rules. Likewise, and with the same shrewdness, they produce specific socio-spatial ecologies. We often believe that calculation only serves to satisfy personal interests based on indicators and quantifiable units of measure. However, when we observe debt dynamics and landscapes we notice that the calculation goes far beyond the economic deal (Weber 2010). These subjects do not try desperately only to make ends meet. On the contrary, they try to establish special individual, family, or group identities. They are part of a series of networks of rights and obligations with which they have to negotiate and which have to sometimes be reinforced or dissolved. Debts either serve multiple and often conflicting purposes, associated with the search for prestige and respectability or, on the contrary, they represent processes of subservience and control. When indebted subjects make economic decisions involving dwelling, they establish precise calculation strategies, thinking tools, and spatial strategies that require the use of multiple cognitive dimensions. Juggling acts that literally involve throwing, catching and "holding things in the air" all at the same time; this requires speed and a search for balance, but also involves taking on risks. Indebted subjects combine several financial tools involving continuous practices regarding loans, reimbursements, and new loans. Loans are taken in one place to repay another elsewhere. In some cases, individuals swap roles as debtors and creditors; sometimes the poorest can also be creditors. Juggling loans, mortgagees and credits is certainly a form of financial calculation in which sustainable debts rotate with others that are more expensive. Juggling debt is undoubtedly also a question of time, because creditors impose different repayment schedules. Social motivation is also important. Permanent tension between an individual and the group, as well as

[32] Rama (1984) maintains that, ever since the colonial era, the construction of space throughout the Latin American continent has been the result of an urban-centric vision in which rural space is considered as the only indigenous place of production subordinate to the city, considered as the one place in which to seek the "good life."

personal aspirations and collective responsibilities, is closely linked to debt and its terms and conditions.

6 In Ecuador

In countries like Ecuador, indebtedness often reflects differences in status and income. In these geographical areas, anyone with assets not only has more of a chance to obtain loans from formal sources, but is also more likely to obtain loans in order to accumulate more assets. On the contrary, those without assets turn primarily to informal sources and are more inclined to obtain a loan to meet their household needs.[33] So it's not surprising that the poor have a debt/net assets ratio higher than the rich. Even if most of the loans in Ecuador come from informal sources, personal loans (especially the ones obtained by women) are more likely to come from informal sources, compared to the ones taken out by couples. Likewise, while the majority of loans are taken out to accrue assets, the loans for which women are individually responsible are more likely to have been taken out so they can buy things (Deere and Catanzarite 2016). Given this framework, increased access to credit thanks to microfinance, for example, reduces the short term effects of poverty, but reproduces dynamics of concentration of wealth that persist in the long term (Esposito 2013).[34] The *Red Financiera Rural* is one of the main promoters of the diffusion of microfinance in Ecuador; it includes private banks, savings and credit

[33] Most quantitative studies about debt in areas of the Global South tend to focus only on entrepreneurs (individual or families) that operate, for example, in agriculture or animal husbandry; the studies also analyze the access to and use of credit only for these specific activities (Fanelli 2011). This is nearly always defined as so-called "productive credit." Nevertheless, families are very often engaged in multiple activities that generate income and can obtain loans from various sources for different purposes. Furthermore, loans can be entered into for one purpose and used for another (Collins 2008). So it is important to move beyond "productive credit" and study the relationship between the distribution of wealth, access to credit, and indebtedness.

[34] Wealth is conventionally defined as the sum total of valuable physical assets (including houses and consumer durables) and financial activities (Davies 2008). In a three-tier financial system, owning physical and financial assets can act as guarantees for loans. For example, while consumer durables are rarely sufficient to act as a guarantee for a private bank loan, a TV, heater, or fridge can be accepted as a guarantee by non-bank institutions and the informal sector, since they can be sold or pawned to repay a debt (Vogelgesang 2003). Furthermore, a cooker or fridge bought in instalments can be used as an independent work tool by women engaged in selling food or drinks, just like car ownership can be a potential means to generate income if used as a taxi or Uber to provide a transport service. Debts for expenses involve the indebtedness incurred to be able to make daily payments, for example, for food or to pay bills, transportation, clothes, school fees, medical bills, or family events. Other reasons include expenses to help family members migrate abroad or repay earlier loans.

cooperatives, and NGOs. These institutions operate in both rural areas and marginal urban contexts; their mission is to foster financial inclusion.[35]

The American dollar became Ecuador's official currency after the financial crisis in 1999–2000. The crisis occurred at the end of a decade of economic instability and was triggered by the collapse of twenty-two commercial banks that held roughly 60% of the activities of the private financial system. Most analysts believe that the instability was due to a combination of excessive deregulation, financial liberalization, high foreign debt, political instability, and instable oil prices—the country's main export (Da Ros 2003; Jácome 2007). In the next 10 years attempts were made to restore trust in the public by rebuilding the public banking system and redefining the regulations governing the private banking system. In 2006, private bank credit as a percentage of the gross domestic product (GDP) was 22%, placing Ecuador below the Latin American average, but above much bigger economies such as Peru and Mexico. In 2010, it had risen to 28% (Fanelli 2011). At present two institutions govern the formal and private financial system: the *Superintendencia de bancos y seguros del Ecuador*, or SBS (Superintendency of Banks and Insurance Companies) that regulates all private commercial banks, and the *Superintendencia de Economía Popular y Solidaria*, or SEPS (Superintendency of Popular and Solidarity Economy) that controls all forms of cooperative financial associations (Superintendencia de Economía Popular y Solidaria 2013, 2014; Deere and Catanzarite 2017). Even if most of the savings and credit cooperatives were established in the 1960s, their numbers have gradually increased throughout the country after the collapse of the bank sector. A 2002 census of the savings cooperatives, banks, and mutual funds revealed that there were twenty-six regulated cooperatives and 350 non-regulated institutions. The latter had over half a million members (Jácome and Cordovéz 2004). The composition of the loan portfolios of the private banks and the savings and loan cooperatives is very different. The former concentrate primarily on commercial sectors and businesses, while the latter are involved in services to micro businesses and families.[36]

As part of an international comparative study, a survey of the assets of families in Ecuador, entitled the *Encuesta Activos FLACSO-Florida* (EAFF), was carried out in 2010 by FLASCO, *Facultad Latinoamericana de Ciencias Sociales* and the University of Florida. The study was based on a sample of 2892 representative families from the coastal regions and plateaus in Ecuador. Its main objective was to assess the assets owned by families and individuals (EAFF 2010).

Seventy percent of the 1791 loans identified by the survey came from formal sources, and 30% from informal sources. In the formal sector, business-credits were the most frequent source of loans, obtained by 14% of families. Generally speaking, these loans were instalment loans to purchase goods or services. Private banks and savings cooperatives were the second most frequent source of loans (9%). Only 2%

[35] A survey of families in Quito, Guayaquil, and Cuenca showed that in 2003 only 12.5% of families had access to a loan the previous year (Jácome 2005). In 2006, the percentage, again referring to the previous year, was 51.5 (Rural Finance Network 2013).

[36] See: the World Bank [online]. https://pip.worldbank.org/country-profiles/ECU.

of families obtained microfinance loans from NGOs and other private lenders, e.g., religious groups. Friends and relatives were the most frequent source of loans from the informal sector. Moneylenders or *chulqueros* were not a very common source of loans, mentioned only by 2% of the families involved in the *FLACSO* survey. Informal loan groups, e.g., rotating savings and credit associations, the so-called *Rosca*, were even less common.[37] The fact very few people turned to moneylenders and informal loan groups reflects the increase in competition due to the growth of microfinance institutions in Ecuador, beginning in the early twenty-first century.[38] As regards gender differences, state banks tend to grant loans mainly to men, while NGOs tend to prefer women. Loans by informal credit groups are more common among women, while loans by employers are usually granted to single men; this reflects the fact that a bigger percentage of men have a formal job compared to women.[39] Out of 1821 loans for a single purpose, 68% were taken out to accumulate assets, and 32% to pay for purchases. This is particularly alarming, because it suggests that the loans used by poor people to buy assets are less likely to generate a future income flow, making reimbursement of the loan potentially very difficult.

There are several reasons why families in Ecuador take out loans. The most frequent are to purchase durable consumer goods (28%) and start a commercial activity (27%). They are followed either by the purchase of a lot or a house, or to improve or enlarge a dwelling (19%), meet daily needs (15%), and pay medical expenses (10%). People who are economically more fragile take out loans either to buy durable consumer goods, i.e., a cooker, a TV or a fridge, or to pay for daily needs and medical issues. On the contrary, richer families take out loans more frequently, either to purchase or modernize their homes, or for commercial activities. The rich are more likely to take out a loan to buy a vehicle, while poorer people tend to take out a loan to pay for education. This interpretation indicates that, compared to

[37] *Rosca* is a term used in several Latin American countries, including Ecuador; it refers to a type of informal savings or collective financing system. It consists of a group of individuals who meet regularly to make set contributions, and in turn each are given the entire sum. For example, if there are ten people in a *Rosca* and every member contributes $100, every month a different member receives $1000. This allows the participants to access a bigger sum of money compared to what they could individually save in the short-term. *Rosca* is based on reciprocal trust between the participants and on participation in a predefined contribution and distribution program. In many cases, this informal method replaces or integrates formal financial institutions, especially for those who may not have access to traditional bank credit.

[38] Overall, loans to couples are more likely to come from formal sources compared to loans for which either one man or one women is responsible. This is partly due to the fact that formal credit sources are more inclined to follow legal regulations and ask that a loan to a married person be co-signed by the spouse. However, loans to couples could also reflect institutional preferences; families with two incomes, for example, are usually considered to deserve more credit (EAFF 2010).

[39] It's useful to note than when women take out loans by themselves, they mostly look for loans from family members, while men turn more to friends as a source for a loan. In addition, data regarding 46 microfinance institutions that are part of the Rural Finance Network (RFR) show that 69% of the clients of NGOs are women, compared to the overall average of members of the RFR (54%) (Rural Finance Network 2013).

poorer families, richer families are more inclined to either incur debts to purchase assets that generate income, or as guarantees for future loans.[40]

Couples are significantly more likely to take out loans to purchase goods; single women tend to become indebted in order to pay for purchases rather than sustain an entrepreneurial activity. While loans to purchase assets are more likely to come from formal loan sources, loans for purchases are more likely to come from informal sources (Schicks 2013b). Furthermore, belonging to a group can increase the chance of finding a guarantor for a loan; in Ecuador this is necessary in order to obtain loans from private banks and most savings cooperatives. Religious groups are the most common groups to which women belong, followed by parents' associations and community groups. Men tend to primarily trust workers' associations and unions, for example, the politically very powerful union of taxi drivers.[41] Being a member of a union reflects the importance of the kind of work a person does, in this case in the formal sector (Mideros 2010).

Generally speaking, men are more likely to obtain loans, receive income from a formal job, belong to a politically important group, and have a current bank account. The latter is crucial in order to obtain a bank mortgage.[42] Associations, corporations, or unions can be more or less politically influential locally, and thus provide different levels of collateral for a loan. The role of social networks to access information about groups and credit institutes is, therefore, very important (Fletschner and Mesbah 2011). However, in Ecuador, this statement is true mostly for men, due to the fact that men and women belong to different kinds of associations.

Family wealth is more important for women than men when they wish to take out a loan. If either a man or woman are not married, they are less likely to be able to take out a loan to purchase assets.[43] In general, families in Ecuador do not appear to be severely in debt; total debt is only 5.8% of total net assets. According to Shorrocks et al. (2012), in countries in the Global South this ratio is usually below 10%. In Ecuador, men are the subjects more likely to "recycle debt," and also declare a "negative net worth." Compared to men (13.5%), a higher percentage of women with "negative net worth" tend to become indebted to cover the reimbursement of other loans (20.2%). This indicates that women are more likely to be caught in a

[40] It is common for private banks and savings cooperatives in Ecuador to ask potential borrowers to have a savings account or maintain a minimum balance in their account since having formal borrowers reduces the need for short-term credit, making the holders of the accounts more inclined to ask for loans to purchase assets (Kast and Pomeranz 2014).

[41] Individuals who are members of a social network or a group have greater access to information about credit availability and conditions, and are therefore more inclined to take out loans for assets (Fletschner and Mesbah 2011).

[42] The main factor positively associated with the ability of men and women to access loans to accumulate assets in Ecuador is for them to be holders of a formal savings account. The relationship between holding a current account in a bank and access to credit has often been cited in literature (Sanguinetti et al. 2011).

[43] It's interesting to note that being in a consensual union, compared to being married, only reduces the possibility for men. Being Afro-Ecuadorian (compared to whites or mixed race) increases the probability, for both men and women, of becoming indebted to purchase assets.

debt trap, i.e., when new debts are incurred to pay back old ones.[44] Even though the formal sector in Ecuador is the primary source of loans, most of the poor turn to informal sources. The latter have the most alarming ratio between debt and net worth, embroiled in a debt loop that is unsustainable in the long run. Women in particular have higher levels of suffering due to debt; this is due to their tendency to become indebted in order to pay back earlier debts (Schicks 2013a). These situations of over-indebtedness are usually considered to be either the result of external political shocks, the behavior of the lender (unsuitable products and procedures), or of the indebted subject.

Many women make work-related decisions based on the logic of indebtedness (Portes and Hoffman 2003). Some start to perform illegal activities, for example, selling food in the streets without a municipal authorization.[45] If a person works in the field of itinerant trade, banks are never a reference institution, because when, for example, that person falls ill, he or she cannot work and therefore cannot repay his/her debt. So it's better to interact with other itinerant sellers rather than the bank. In addition, establishing a relationship with the bank means being registered in the so-called *Central de riesgo*, or risk center.[46]

As in other countries, in Ecuador the financialization of popular economies satisfies, interprets, and intercepts a desire for autonomy, economic independence, and the construction of self. The action of debt in social reproduction processes, especially in feminized economies, reveals the value of historically devalued, underpaid, and invisibilized activities. Ultimately, it is a special moralization model used to limit and contain challenges to gender mandates in social reproductive tasks. Finance works along these lines, trying to use debt to turn precarious unemployed

---

[44] "Recycling debt" is an expression used to describe a financial activity in which an existing debt is either restructured or extended using new loans of financing. In general, this practice is undertaken to pay an existing debt using a new loan; often the objective is to obtain more favorable conditions, such as lower interest rates or more advantageous reimbursement terms. "Negative net worth" occurs when a person or a company has a total net value below zero. In short, it indicates that liabilities (debts, financial obligations, etc.) exceed the assets of that person or company (investments, financial resources, etc.).

[45] Quite a few women choose not to sign up to social security; they believe it takes away more resources than it provides. Many others think that low-income labor (i.e., unqualified formal female labor) produces less income compared to independent informal labor. This situation questions the reasons why, in those contexts, they end up being treated in private clinics, or why they presume there will be no pension and, therefore, believe there are no benefits in contributing to social security. In a nutshell, the credit office, the police, and the *Central de Riesgo* [Centre of Risk] are three elements that influence the dynamics of Ecuadorian popular economies.

[46] The *Central de Riesgo* is an entity or database that records and preserves information regarding the debt granted to individuals and companies by financial institutions, such as banks and credit societies. Its ultimate purpose is to let financial institutions assess the credit risk of an applicant by checking his/her credit rating over a period of time. This tool helps banks take informed decisions when assessing new requests for a loan or financing. It is important to note that the information filed in the *Central de Riesgo* can influence the ability of a person or company to obtain further financing; so it is crucial to maintain a good position in this system in order to have access to credit. In Ecuador the *Central de Riesgo* is run by the *Dirección Nacional de Registro de Datos Públicos.*

figures into "self-employed female workers," i.e., female entrepreneurs. Women are redefined by the language of finance as "natural" entrepreneurs, responsible debtors, or compulsive consumers.

The last crises sparked an intense, violent increase in reproductive work: care for the education of children in the family, care-giving, and an increase in requests for cleaning and teleworking. This increase in reproductive work has paradoxically generated more debt. Unacknowledged housework turns into unequal income which, in turn, becomes a further source of indebtedness. This situation is also directly linked to the growth of economies and forms of illegal labor in situations of social vulnerability, thus contributing to an increase in violent situations, both in the home and city. The financial colonization of social production turns precarious impoverished populations into territories to be conquered, making them dependent on debt. In Ecuador, when the debt ratio declined, the trickle-down effects on the national public debt spread like wildfire. In other words, the expropriations and privatizations triggered by the national debt turned into a compulsive indebtedness vis-à-vis subaltern sectors that increasingly accessed goods and services through the mediation of debt (Deere and Contreras 2011). This modified the debt-to-income ratio, but also the ratio between debt and access to rights. Life turns into a summation of debts: personal debts and the sums paid in relation to public debt.

Indebtedness, even in countries like Ecuador, is not only a response to social struggles and a desire for independence, but also a mechanism to exploit the labor and extraction of a person's life time. We can call it financial extractivism, insofar as it highlights the forms of extraction of value performed by debt practices, without wage mediation, on multiple heterogeneous forms of the contemporary labor force. Being obliged to be in debt, i.e., the mandate that leaves a person no choice but to become indebted, proves that debt acts as a productive tool. It makes people work, forcing them to work more and more. Above all, debt as a device for the production of the self configures the spaces and ecologies of dwelling.

7 The Intimate Dimension of Debt

The considerations presented in this essay illustrate the fact that debt is not something limited to the relationship between economies, finance, "development," and society, but instead is an element that acts within phenomena of intensification of social, gender, and racial inequalities, as well as many forms of environmental and climatic injustices.[47] In particular, in the so-called Global South, the most interesting places to study in order to identify the manifestations, dimensions, and

[47] In particular, something is changing in the way in which architecture and urban planning currently view phenomena such as climate change or the defense of the environment. The time has come to "acclimatize" social conflict and politicize climate and environment conflict. In this respect, the notion of debt can be useful in defining new operational modes and new design solutions. This is the hypothesis put forward by Patel (2010, 2012) who encourages us to reason, for

socio-spatial implications of the indebtedness of subjects and families appear to be the neighborhoods and parts of cities usually considered as politically, spatially, and financially peripheral or marginal. In these contexts, indebtedness, especially household debt, is explicitly visible and reflected in urban spaces and set ups. Therefore we need to stand on the threshold between the economy, dwelling, and spatial production processes and observe certain specific spaces, boundaries and "interiors" of debt as well as the spatial practices, processes of subservience, and ruses used by indebted individual or collective subjects to negotiate and resist debt. Obviously there are multiform situations and experiences of debt, corresponding to the processes of production of dwelling spaces in which the various forms and sources of indebtedness tend to be combined. These considerations illustrate the links established between debt interpreted as an economic relationship and as spatial production processes. If we are unable to understand the different kinds of values, desires and conflicts embodied by objects, buildings, and the spaces of debt, we will be unable to understand the reasons why vulnerable subjects accept indebtedness in order to live in a marginal and precarious neighborhood. Debt is considered both a form of predation and an extractive process (Graeber 2011; Lebaron 2014) countering the dominant conception that sees debt through the lens of financial inclusion and the promotion of individual enterprise. Debt is also used to define forms of resistance to neo-colonial and extractive processes. Strategies of resistance and "escape" from debt emerge based on astute strategies to produce dwelling spaces, redefined as structures to capture resources, and as infrastructures to support instable and rooted dwelling. Those who live in debt know how to nestle in it, "cannibalizing it," and twisting its logic in their favor. They are the real experts who know how to proceed, even though they often do not have the resources to structurally construct their solution.[48]

The architecture of debt is affective in nature; it acts during different moments of emotional tensions, for example, a state of desperation or moments of desire or satisfaction. There are intense moments (the reminder sent by the bank, a meeting with the financial advisor) that emerge as part of a general "background noise" during which people are involved in continuous self-assessments. Indebted individuals are often people who are overwhelmed, exhausted, hopeful, and resigned. Their indebted lives are colored by relationships of obligation and co-dependence coupled with affective and often conflictual states (e.g., hyper-vigilance, dissociation, and anxiety) that emerge within a general "background noise" (Stewart 2007; Berlant and Stewart 2019). In her book *Cruel Optimism* (2011), Lauren Berlant focused on these low-intensity modes of affection. She discusses, in particular, three affective domains: "hyper-vigilance," "slow death," and "escape." "Hyper-vigilance" is

---

example, on topics such as climate change and food self-sufficiency; he considers debt to be a key issue, and not the search for techno-optimistic solutions.

[48] During the studies, the interviewees did not always speak about their life problems in terms of debt, although they did admit that it was a constant in their lives. They were more inclined to mention working conditions, bad social relations, or a precarious political situation as the source of their problems.

considered to be a psychological state in which the subject constantly focuses on how his/her attention is deviated toward imageries of prosperity (publicity images). The "slow death" concept describes an operational space and an abandonment marked by practices that alleviate the stress of an exhausted life (eating, having sex, "distancing oneself"). Hyper-vigilance and the continuous pressure of an austere life ultimately create the conditions that lead to the search for suspension or "escape" from the "background noise," either by choosing to travel and having experiences, or making special social, affective or spiritual choices not in line with self-discipline practices. All these affective states are incorporated into the debt cycle. So, in contrast with the story by Maurizio Lazzarato, in an indebted life there is much more than the practices of self-discipline and regularization of time that would constitute indebted subjectivization. Moments of escape and suspension exist. As do moments of resistance. All this means that debt is not only space, but that the body also becomes porous and insecure, permeated by tensions that come from several subjects, such as creditors, the family and relatives, as well as from several imageries, for example from the desire for a good, respectable urban life.

The ensuing chapters contain a comparison between several spaces and events that took place in the Ecuadorian cities of Quito (Solanda and Carapungo neighborhoods) and Loja (neighborhoods of Ciudad Victoria and Los Geranios). Based on these spaces and events it is possible to present certain considerations about the spatial nature of debt and the links between desires for emancipation, forms of subservience, and value extraction processes. The considerations focus on the notion of incrementalism and porosity.

7.1 Incrementalism

The first issue involves the relationship between indebtedness and the incremental process to produce a habitat. For indebted subjects, the house is considered as a means and an infrastructure to sustain ways to try and defuse the violence of debt. The production of dwelling spaces and structures through debt spatially turns into incremental processes. Buildings are seen as open-ended, something that can be enlarged based on the possibilities and dimensions of the incurred debts. Incremental construction corresponds to a process of interactions and reciprocal adaptation between multiple actors with different and often conflictual needs that change over time. As described by Lindblom (1957, 1959) incrementalism accentuates confrontation with contingent problems, in this case with problems involving the enlargement of the house. Ordinary solutions are often used for the interiors, and the main investment nearly always involves technological devices. Instead the exterior is modeled and given highly symbolic finishes: bay windows shaped like little temples, diversely shaped moldings, and pilaster strips. Finally, the house is no longer seen as a traditional domestic space, but as an incremental infrastructure supporting the lives of families that are sometimes extended families, networks of relatives living in many different cities and rural areas. It is a structure that helps to establish links between several economies, subjects, and sources of income. The family can gain new members, but can also lose them, and displace them. The same is true for objects; household furniture and appliances can be purchased, but also exchanged, sold, moved, and replaced. Indeed, coexistence between subjects belonging to the same family nucleus and lodgers in the same house generates a special social and physical structure of the house, i.e., divided into small intimate rooms and collective rooms; the house is reconfigured as an urban device combining the private, intimate dimension of dwelling and the public, social dimension of the neighborhood. In the words of Morton and Boyer (2021) the family becomes an "hyposubject" with a structure which, thanks to the increase in exchanges between its members, tends to be all the more stable, the more it is complex.[49] The end product is a mix between forms of stable rooted dwelling by some of the subjects who live continuously in the house, and temporary dwelling by individuals who reside in the house for a few months or years, either due to their job or because they are studying. The house is no longer a traditional domestic space but a stratified object, a space in which, for example, there are work areas, commercial spaces, or rooms to rent; the whole house is redefined as an infrastructure used to accrue the additional economic resources necessary to contrast debt.

The infrastructure concept has recently acquired a key role in urban and dwelling studies (Appel et al. 2018). Berlant (2016), for example, describes infrastructure not only as a socio-material system ordering and organizing social actions and practices, but also as a dynamic device sustaining social life, actions, and practices. To recognize and consider something as an infrastructure one has to look at how they either support or are crossed by social, economic, and political practices and processes, making the action possible in special ways. Infrastructures are relational devices that exist only as part of a relationship with something else; their ontology resides in being both things and relationships between things (Boyer 2018; Larkin 2013). This means that infrastructures are such when they "do" something in the socio-spatial world; as such, they should be analyzed in relation to the way in which they order and organize space and dwelling. Infrastructures "press the flesh" (Fennell 2015, p. 32); they are generative devices, points of contact between broad social processes, structures, and everyday life. Considering the house as an infrastructure involves highlighting the possibilities provided by its spaces and structure. Infrastructures order and create differences. In this respect, the form and spatial layout of houses are both a product and a device to produce power relations. Infrastructures order and organize this difference thanks to the experiences and practices of the people who live in them, thus reflecting differences in identity, gender, and social standing.

---

[49] A hyposubject, a term invented by Timothy Morton, is a concept referring to the relationship between a subject and his surroundings. Morton argues that entities are interconnected and interdependent rather than separate or distant from their environment. The hyposubject suggests a vision of existence in which there is no clear-cut separation between the subject and the external environment, but that there is more of a continuity or intertwining between them.

7.2 Porosity

In places that financially colonize the habitat, not only does the house become a work space, it also turns into a factory producing big urban areas, redefined as vast domestic territories. With reference, once again, to the issue of reproductive labor, we must necessarily consider not only what is performed inside the houses, but also certain activities that are performed in several urban structures in the neighborhood. Some houses are turned into kindergartens; *comedores* or collective canteens are created, as well as work spaces, shared ateliers, *canchas*, and systems of open spaces that act as "social condensers." Roads and facilities such as schools are repaired thanks to the joint work of the *minga*.[50]

Examples of externally deployed reproductive work also exist. Activities such as education, medical assistance, care and services to the person, and in some cases small agro-ecological productions are reorganized in the neighborhood which, due to these phenomena, tends to become a domestic space. This appears to create a continuum that challenges the division between public and private and turns into an externalization of domesticity. During this process, household chores are shifted outside; at the same time, the house absorbs the productive dynamics previously performed externally. Neighborhood community networks sustain, intervene, take care of, and, in some cases, prevent the neighborhood from becoming violent. It is mainly women who work in this dimension of opaque labor, hidden like domestic labor. This kind of work deals with either everyday—food, medical issues—or emergencies created by gender violence and dwelling hardships (Ananya 2010; Sparke et al. 2012; Gago 2020). The special relationship between conditions of porosity and the traits of domesticity—characterizing many spaces of the habitat produced through debt—makes it possible to pinpoint conditions of urban porosity that are very different to the situations of interconnection, interaction, and intertwining between open and closed spaces that Walter Benjamin attributed to Mediterranean urban contexts like Naples. The spatial porosity produced by debt is the result of the extension of domesticity from the scale of the house to that of the neighborhood which tends, one way or another, to be redefined as a big urban interior.

8 Design and Debt: Feminist Actions of Resistance

In general, the settings of debt could be described, on the one hand, as the result of the tension between a demand for space and services and, on the other, an inability or denial to grant them. Lack is what embodies debt. The result of the negotiation of

[50] In Ecuador, the Quechan term *minga* refers to a cultural tradition of collaborative and community work. Minga is a custom in which community members come together either to do collective work, such as constructing roads and buildings, or performing other useful activities for the community; its usefulness is not directly enjoyed by those who perform it.

insufficiency through debt is naturalization, the neutralization of the demand and, at the same time, the spark behind processes that produce a type of informal urban space marked by violence and creativity, conflict, and solidarity. So, the city of debt is productive. Production consists in the ability to invent spatial structures and human links, movements of individuals, and cooperation. The face of these productive figures is nearly always that of women, because it is women who, in a space increasingly colonized by finance, develop ideas, forms, and actions of resistance, as well as the "torsion" of debt. As far back as 1999, the feminist sociologist Maria Mies noted that in some countries in the south, the nascent subsistence economies were chiefly organized by women, and that these economies consolidated forms of social cohesion. Mies wrote that if the direct production of food provided by women are added to "all the other varied forms of subsistence work—food preparation, bartering with food [… helping others, fetching and carrying water, then it becomes evident that the survival of the majority of people in these cities depends on women's subsistence work" (Mies and Bennhold-Thomsen 1999, p. 127). Since the late 1990s, these phenomena have become more pronounced; they have been fueled by consistent and persistent country-to-city migration processes, chiefly in places like Latin America. Even in the suburbs of small Latin-American cities, whether in planned areas or areas occupied due to collective action processes, in the middle of a decades-long economic crisis women appeared to be the ones more capable of establishing several political economies and different forms of social reproduction, thus detecting process of resistance to debt and social demands.

So what should be done when houses and urban spaces become the target of financial capital, reconfigured as spaces of control, subservience, and the production of value?

What strategies and forms of design are possible in and against debt?

Separation and social fragmentation is a normal state of affairs in Latin-American societies. However, it is also true that the main action of debt is to hold together what is divided by promoting specific imaginaries of dwelling, and by configuring structures of dwelling that are about to collapse. So the best option is to operate within these logics, cannibalizing them and twisting them until debt is turned against them. Design must therefore act in those areas where it becomes impossible to prevent unity, where it is possible to block the mechanism of synthesis, up to the limits of rupture and possibly beyond. This point is inside the indebted subject, above all a female indebted subject, as the latter is inside the debt. Being inside, acting against, getting out. The work produced by indebted subjects, in particular by women, is worth double in the debt system: once as the force that produces it, and again as the force that refuses to produce it. Once inside the debt, and once against the debt.

Now that we are "in" these forms of social demand and strategies of resistance to rational debt we need to operationally rethink them as strategies of design capable of providing points of resistance to the subservience produced by debt. The three possible strategies of design listed below are based on the identification of certain spatial traits of debt. Design strategies capable of tackling the dynamics of debt are presented based on narratives which, metaphorically, recall the plots of films or TV series. In films, the narrative is a way to examine certain current conditions, sometimes by exacerbating its traits and providing another interpretation. It can be an excellent way to develop a design concept in line with the spatial traits and dynamics of debt.

Breaking Bad

Two people create an illegal chemical lab to produce methamphetamine inside a camper. They want to sell the drugs on the black market. They completely transform the space inside the vehicle, getting rid of most of the objects that would turn it into a domestic space. The fact they need to work in a place where they have to hide what they are doing makes the domestic space of the camper ideal, because its shell automatically links the activity inside this vehicle to a very precise idea of domesticity, far from their work, especially their illegal work. However, they keep several little domestic elements that allow them to live in it. Since the lab is inside the camper, it is also mobile. They can shift their production anywhere the market is favorable. The camper as a spatial structure helps their illegal activity, since it is hermetically closed off from the world around it, with curtains and shutters; it uses mechanical mechanisms to pump out the air full of toxic substances and make the interior liveable.

The first way to resist debt through design is to turn the dwelling into an infrastructure with which to gain more resources and, at the same time, create a satisfactory situation of comfort for its inhabitants. The "productive house" is an incremental structure shaped by logistical motives and linked to the orbital movements of the subjects that live in it; it is also a platform that can be used to forge economies and incomes. The reference is to the integration of formal income with revenue from small commercial activities or the rent paid for the use of rooms created inside the house. In many cases, the house is a laboratory, a place where women perform informal work. Above all, it is a sealed space. The closure of patios, courtyards, and gardens to create bigger living rooms helps to define interiors designed as collective spaces, places for supportive exchanges rather than family intimacy. The house considered as an infrastructure or platform supporting these forms of dwelling becomes a spatially very complex object, the materialization of traditional domestic rooms, shared spaces, and parts of semi-independent houses. These solutions help tackle what some authors call *desarrollo divergente* or the "divaricating" growth of an extended family group in which there are rooted figures and other pieces of furniture.[51] All this raises, in a novel manner, the question of designing incremental dwellings, of designing the house as a stratified infrastructure in which to piece together traditional domestic rooms and structures to confine and produce resources. This strategy alludes to the configuration of changeable, introvert, and incremental

[51] The concept of development or *desarrollo divergente*, usually employed in the field of economic studies, is used in the field of urban studies by Ignacio de Teresa Fernández-Casas to describe forms of dwelling in which individuals cohabit inside the same house, establishing stable and cohesive relationships regarding certain aspects of family life and seeking conditions of independence in others (Fernández-Casas 2016).

dwelling spaces, considered as an ensemble of intimate spaces, of semi-collective rooms, and rooms in which to work. This is the *Breaking Bad* form of dwelling.

The Martian

NASA sends six astronauts to explore the planet Mars for a year; they settle into a "HAB", a domestic space divided into two independent rooms. There is a rectangular area where they can rest and care for themselves, and a bigger space, shaped like a dodecahedron; its perimeter is completely equipped with a kitchen, a computer, storage space, a hanger for their space suits, and the control panels they need to maintain the habitat. The internal space of the dodecahedron is full of mobile furniture on wheels, so that it can be moved to anywhere in the habitat. During the film, one of the astronauts is forced to survive for years on the planets while waiting for a rescue mission to reach him. He creates a field where he plants potatoes. To make sure they grow, he needs to create an atmosphere inside the habitat with a specific temperature and humidity.

The second form of resistance, at neighborhood level, is linked to the activation of neighborhood assemblies and collectives connected to the spatial configuration of informal market spaces, *comedores populares*, *merenderos*, and collective canteens. These urban structures are places that witness the rise of a counter-power of the forces of extractive finance, allowing residents not only to survive, but also develop new forms of relationships and social exchange. As stated by the Uruguayan activist and social theorist Raúl Zibechi (2012), it is chiefly in these rooms that women make sure that everyday life goes on; it is in these rooms that new relationships develop, providing not only basic services, but also changing the way in which social reproduction and the production of space are organized. María Galindo, member of the anarchic-female organization in Bolivia, Mujeres Creando (2009), maintains that debt has led to a break in and dilution of the urban space of domestic chores, producing a culture of resistance. Galindo (2013) emphasizes that the image of women shut in the house is a thing of the past, because to fight precarious labor and the economic crises linked to the proliferation of debt, women in particular have taken over the streets and their flows, turning them into means of subsistence, into spatial structures of residence and self-support, where they spend most of their time. Markets, *canchas*, and pavements are places where you can be stopped by the police who control your documents, but they are also spaces in which to try and redefine networks of mutual support and solidarity, a place where you can dispel the isolation of household chores. To think about the design of these structures, considered as social condensers, as introvert urban interiors in which several functions are associated and superimposed, corresponds to *The Martian* form of dwelling.

Amores Perros

Three stories interconnected in an ostensibly unconscious manner. Octavio is in love with his sister-in-law. To win a large sum of money and run away with her he decides to enter his brother's dog in a clandestine dogfight. A model and an assassin are the protagonists of the other two stories. The model is going through a period of profound crisis in her working life and with her partner after she lost a leg during an accident; she also has a problem with her dog. The gangster prefers to remain alone in bare, dirty rooms and share his intimacy with dogs rather than with human beings and his family. The suburbs is the place where people fight to survive existentially and physically. The block where Octavio lives is a series of houses and dirty apartments; the setting is visually intense and violent, with compressed and dilated spaces hosting a humanity immersed in an abyssal, ferocious solitude.

The third form of resistance can be defined by recalling the German word *kunstwollen*, a concept that describes the will to turn a social, economic, and cultural fact into an image. *Debtscapes* are easy to recognize visually. Their style is characterized by extensive moldings, pediments that look like small temples, a medley of bay windows, and colored French windows. These ensembles are more or less codified and repetitive. From a visual point of view, the neighborhoods of debt are seemingly disorderly and, basically, monotonous. Spaces of boredom, control, and projection of the identity of a social group. In other words, domestic spaces. It involves the production of a language purposely distant from the languages that are the result of a pure technical and constructive rationale. The intent is similar to a political decision. But the decision is never personal, never private or secret; it is determined by the accumulation of multiple emotional states, tensions, pains, tactics, and reactions to debt that the inhabitants who live here implement by adopting an architectural language that has become consolidated as a common norm. In the scenes of *Ciudad Victoria*, this multitude becomes uniqueness, a creating totality. In many ways, it involves *splicing*, sampling, and remixing images produced using a technique that could, for example, be the *photobashing* technique. The result is the configuration of landscapes and layouts of dwelling, marked by a *queer* attitude that threatens current binary orders dominated by traditional family values, by an inducement toward economic growth anchored to an interminable present. The result is the creation of *debt futurism*, collectively geared toward an incremental rather than explosive spatial change.[52] This is the *Amores Perros* form of dwelling.

By exploiting these forms of resistance it may be possible to try and operate "inside" the debt, absorbing and twisting it in one's favor, challenging codes and intentions that basically consider the house and urban space as a resource at the service of the valorization of capital. The space produced by these forms of resistance combines private dimensions with collective resources; it becomes a device of resistance and a tool to express a form of antagonism. These forms of resistance to debt can be considered as decolonial, feminist operations, as forms of a design discourse that must be urgently structured. When reflecting on debt and trying to assume a clear design-oriented approach, it is important to challenge a complex mindset regarding the creditor/debtor relationships, since in the life and space of

[52] In contemporary art and the cinema, ideas about divergent futures are crystallized in forms of so-called ethno-futurisms, for example, *Tropical Futurism*, *Sinofuturism*, *Indigenous Futurism*, and *Afrofuturism.* Many of them present alternative scenarios to western progress, either based on the revision of history or on the re-imagination of geopolitics. *Indigenous Futurism* and *Afrofuturism,* for example, ask what science, technology, and industry would be if they did not depend on extractive processes? Others, such as *Sinofuturism* or *Gulf Futurism*, ask how we would see the future if the fundamental concepts of "progress" came from a place that was not the West.

debt there is much more than the self-discipline practices normally associated with indebted subjectivization. The studies performed in Quito and Loja prove that by skirting the restrictions imposed by debt produces layouts and structures that "cannibalize" debt, configuring what could be called "infrastructures of failure." Failure is a break in a transition, a nonlinear displacement between two phases or events. This intentional break produces friction. It reveals an infrastructural "malfunction." The settings of debt are therefore shaped not only by violence in the processes of the distribution of resources and in social and affective relationships, but also by malfunctions or breaks in its operational logic. It's interesting to try and understand how this condition can generate new forms of "rupture" from the inside. "Failure" provides the potential for new organizations of life and dwelling, for new conditions of coexistence between social, economic, and ecological differences. So, to imagine the architectural and urban planning project in these situations means to reason by exploiting infrastructures and spatial devices that ironically distort the extractive logic of debt. It means redefining the meaning and significance of terms like domesticity, infrastructure, public, private, and independence. The objective is the search for spaces and opaque, interrupted and dependent relations, considered as new fundamental qualities of coexistence based on the condition of subservience, rupture, and ruin, linked to debt.

8.1 Stop Children, What's that Sound?

The opening sequence in the film *Lord of War* (2005), directed by Andrew Niccol, with the soundtrack *For What It's Worth* by the Buffalo Springfield band (*Stop Children, What's That Sound?*) is shot from the point of view of a bullet which, from a weapons factory somewhere in eastern Europe, hits the head of a child soldier in a war zone in Africa. The film tells the story of a Ukrainian-born arms dealer from New York who becomes involved in the civil war in Lebanon, gets into business with the Colombian drug cartels and becomes involved in the pillage and plundering performed by Liberian warlords. This three-minute sequence is an example of a trend in contemporary film scripts in which the film's narrative structure acts as a "parasite" compared to the movements of a certain object. It is an example of *it-narrative* script associated with what we now call *hyperlink cinema*.[53]

In the 1980s, Terence Hopkins and Immanuel Wallerstein coined the term *commodity chain* to describe the characteristics of the network of labor and production of a product. Numerous studies have since been carried out on specific goods chains, not only reconstructing the path from production to consumption, but

[53] *Hyperlink* films have multi-linear plots; part of the film's *suspense* is created by the fact that spectators ask themselves how the narratives of the characters are intertwined or intersected. In these market chain films, the narrative link is the relationship that the characters have with a specific product, whether it be weapons, cocaine, or oil.

conceptualizing what these chains reveal about the structure and dynamics of contemporary capitalism.

In many ways, the considerations presented here recall these *it-narratives* assembled as micro-stories. The analysis focuses on a specific type of goods: the domestic debt (especially its multifaceted ramifications and the effects it has on dwellings) and its social nature (concentrating not only on how complicated it is to calculate, but also on the ensemble of its practices, processes, and physical meanings). The analysis explores the ways in which the flows of resources are saved and used in processes to produce a habitat, not only by highlighting the features and problems of the ensuing spatial ecologies and taking into account the humming of the myriads of molecular actions produced by the indebted subjects and collectives, but also by listening to the sound of debt. In short, these considerations address an important issue: how to develop the design project and housing during this contemporary crisis; they identify a field of research defined by the superimposition between finance, architectural project, and urban studies, providing new input into the current debates on the forms and possibilities of a counter-project, far removed from the narratives of resistance, climatic change, and ecological transition. These three words currently echo like a mantra in our discourses about how to consider design during a period of crisis. However, environmental disasters, or the other kinds of crises that occur today, cannot be considered separate from the ever-increasing processes of indebtedness, because debt is one of the major elements behind the "ignition" of the crisis and not one of its effect. Debt, dependence, and domesticity are therefore key terms in a research agenda focusing on how to design a counter-project of co-existence between different subjects, collectives, ecologies and practices of spatial production. First and foremost, concentrating on space through debt. Like an X-ray, this exposes the entire fabric.

Finally, one last consideration.

The mapping and spatial interpretations of debt can help develop design options and identify the drivers behind possible socio-spatial transformations; they can also highlight the limits of our actions and imagination. This impression is not incorrect. The fact we have to face the hard truth that someone, that "we", can be a limit, may also be beneficial. If debt is really a relationship, then it is not a relationship we can abandon, given that all its contradictions pass through the entire social body, including us. When the English director Patrick Keiller talked about the gentrification of certain neighborhoods in London (2013) he ironically noted that any critical study of the topographies and spaces of subservience is always and also, to a certain extent, the observation of collective and personal defeats we sometimes even enjoy. This is not unusual in people who have the privilege of maintaining a foothold when rocked by waves of expropriation. To a certain extent we are those contradictions.

Competing Interest The author of this chapter declares that he has no financial, institutional, or personal conflicts of interest that could have influenced is selection, editing, or publication.

References

Aalbers M (2016) The financialization of housing: a political economy approach. Routledge, London
Aalbers M (2017) The variegated financialization of housing. Int J Urban Reg Res 41(4):542–554
Acosta A (2016) Las dependencias del extractivismo: aporte para un debate incomplete. Aktuel Marx 20:1–22
Alami I (2023) Ten theses on the new state capitalism and its futures. Environ Plan A Econ Space 55(3):764–769
Alami I, Dixon A (2020) The strange geographies of the 'new' state capitalism. Polit Geogr 82:102237
Ananya R (2010) Poverty capital: microfinance and the making of development. Routledge, London
Anzaldúa G (1987) Borderlands/La Frontera: The New Mestiza. San Francisco: Aunt Lute Books
Appadurai A (1996) Modernity at large: cultural dimensions of globalization. University of Minnesota Press, Minneapolis
Appel H, Anand N, Gupta A (2018) Temporality, politics and the promise of infrastructure. In: The promise of infrastructure. Duke University Press, Durham
Arrighi G, Silver B (2001) Caos e governo del mondo. Come cambiano le egemonie e gli equilibri planetari, Mimesi, Milano
Atwood M (2008) Payback: debt and the shadow side of debt. Bloomsbury Publishing, London
Avallone G (2018) Debito privato, debito pubblico e diritto all'abitare. Il debito come rapporto di comando. https://effimera.org/debito-privato-debito-pubblico-diritto-allabitare-debito-rapporto-comando-gennaro-avallone/. Accessed 15 November 2024
Bastiaensen J et al (2013) After the Nicaraguan non-payment crisis: alternatives to microfinance narcissism. Dev Chang 44:4
Bear L, Ho K, Yanagisako S, Lowenhaupt Tsing A (2015) Gens: a feminist manifesto for the study of capitalism. https://culanth.org/fieldsights/652-gens-a-feminist-manifesto-for-the-study-of-capitalism. Accessed 3 February 2024
Berlant L (2011) Cruel optimism. Duke University Press, Durham
Berlant L (2016) The commons: infrastructures for troubling times. Environ Plan D Soc Space 34:393–419
Berlant L, Stewart K (2019) The hundreds. Duke University Press, Durham
Bersani M (2017) Dacci oggi il nostro debito quotidiano. Strategie dell'impoverimento di massa. DeriveApprodi, Roma
Bhattacharya T (2017) Social reproduction theory: remapping class. Recentering Oppression, London
Bourdieu P (1977) Outline of a theory of practice. Cambridge University Press, Cambridge
Boyer D (2018) Infrastructure, potential energy, revolution. In: Appel H, Anand N, Gupta A (eds) The promise of infrastructure. Duke University Press, Durham, pp 223–244
Butler J (2011) Bodies in alliance and the politics of the street. https://transversal.at/transversal/1011/butler/en. Accessed 12 April 2022
Christophers B (2015) The limits to financialization. Dialog Hum Geogr 5(2):183–200
Collins D (2008) Debt and household finance: evidence from the financial diaries. Dev South Afr 25(4):469–479
D'Alessio G, Iezzi S (2016) Over-indebtedness in Italy: how widespread and persistent is it? In: Questioni di Economia e Finanza, n. 319/2016. Banca d'Italia, Roma. https://www.questionegiustizia.it/rivista/articolo/il-sovraindebitamento-alcune-riflessioni-su-cause-effetti-e-possibili-rimedi_673.php. Accessed 3 April 2022
Da Ros GS (2003) El crédito rural y las cooperativas financieras en el Ecuador. Rev UNIRCOOP 1(1):26–139
Datta K, Aznar C (2019) The space-times of migration and debt: re-positioning migrants' debt and credit practices and institutions in, and through, London. Geoforum 98:300–308
Davies J (2008) An overview of personal wealth. In: Davies J (ed) Personal wealth from a global perspective. Oxford University Press, Oxford

Davis M (2006) Planet of slums. Verso, New York
De la Torre A, Ize A, Schmukler S (2011) Financial development in Latin America and the Caribbean: the road ahead. World Bank, Washington
Deere CD, Catanzarite ZB (2016) Measuring the intra-household distribution of wealth in Ecuador: qualitative insights and quantitative outcomes. In: Lee F, Conin B (eds) Handbook of research methods and applications in heterodox economics. Edward Elgar, Cheltenham
Deere C, Catanzarite Z (2017) Who borrows to accumulate assets? Class, gender and indebtedness in Ecuador's credit market. CEPAL 122:108–126
Deere C, Contreras J (2011) Acumulación de activos: una apuesta por la equidad. FLACSO-Ecuador, Quito. http://genderassetgap.org. Accessed 11 June 2023
Deleuze G (1990) Post-scriptum sur les sociétés de contrôle, Pourparlers (1972–1990). Minuit, Paris, pp 240–247
Denning M (2011) The fetishism of debt. http://socialtextjournal.org/periscope_article/the_fetishism_of_debt. Accessed 26 June 2023
Derrida J (1992) Given time: I. Counterfeit money. University of Chicago Press, Chicago
Derudder B, Taylor P (2020) Three globalizations shaping the twenty-first century: understanding the new world geography through its cities. Ann Am Assoc Geogr 110(6):1831–1854
Devlin R, French-Davis R (1995) The great Latin American debt crisis: a decade of asymmetric adjustment. Braz J Polit Econ 15(3):117–142
di Campli A, Gabbianelli A (2022) Delinking. Lo spazio della coesistenza. Letteraventidue, Siracusa
EAFF (2010) Encuesta Activos FLACO-Florida. http://www.flacsoandes.edu.ec/pagina/60759-documentos-de-encuesta-activos-flacso-florida. Accessed 5 giugno 2024
Eagleton-Pierce M (2023) Uncovering the City of London corporation: territory and temporalities in the new state capitalism. EPA Econ Space 55:184–200
Esposito R (2013) Due. La macchina della teologia politica e il posto del pensiero. Einaudi, Torino
Fama M (2017) Il governo della povertà ai tempi della (micro)finanza. Ombre Corte, Verona
Fanelli J (2011) Domestic financial development in Latin Americas. In: Ocampo JA, Ros J (eds) The Oxford handbook of Latin American economics. Oxford University Press, Oxford
Federici S (2011) Calibán y la bruja. Mujeres, cuerpo y acumulación originaria. Tinta Limón, Buenos Aires
Federici S (2019) Social reproduction theory: history, issues and present challenges. Radic Philos 204:55–57
Federici S (2020) Revolution at point zero: housework, reproduction, and feminist struggle. PM Press, Oakland
Federici S, Austin A (2017) Wages for housework. The New York committee 1972–1977: history, theory, documents. Autonomedia, New York
Federici S, Cavallero L, Gago (2021) ¿Quién le debe a quién?: ensayos transnacionales de desobediencia financiera. Tinta Limón, Buenos Aires
Fennell C (2015) Last project standing: civics and sympathy in post-welfare Chicago. University of Minnesota Press, Minnesota. https://www.upress.umn.edu/book-division/books/last-project-standing. Accessed 28 September 2023
Fernández-Casas I (2016) Aproximaciones familia-casa. La vivienda informal consolidada en Santa María de las Lomas. Guayaquil DEARQ 19:30–43
Ferraro V, Rosser M (1994) Global debt and third world development. In: Klare M (ed) World security: challenges for a new century. St. Martin's Press, New York, pp 332–355
Fields D, Uffer S (2013) The financialisation of rental housing. Urban Stud 53(7):1486–1502
Figueroa A (2011) Income inequality and credit markets. CEPAL Rev 105:37–51
Fletschner D, Mesbah D (2011) Gender disparity in access to information: do spouses share what they know? World Dev 39(8):422–1433
Floro M, Messier J (2006) Tendencias y patrones de crédito entre hogares urbanos pobres en Ecuador. In: Herrera G (ed) La persistencia de la desigualdad: género, trabajo y pobreza en América Latina. CONAMU/FLACSO-Ecuador, Quito. https://biblio.flacsoandes.edu.ec/libros/digital/49278.pdf. Accessed 4 March 2023

Foucault M (2008) The birth of biopolitics: lectures at the Collége de France. Palgrave Macmillan, New York, pp 1978–1979
Fraser N (2014) Behind Marx's hidden abode. New Left Rev 86:55–72
Gago V (2017) Neoliberalism from below: popular pragmatics and baroque economies. Duke University Press, Durham
Gago V (2020) Feminist international: how to change everything. Verso, London
Gago V (2022) La potenza femminista. O il desiderio di cambiare tutto. Capovolte, Alessandria
Gago V, Cavallero L (2019) Una lectura feminista de la deuda. Fundación Rosa Luxemburg, Buenos Aires
Gago V, Cavallero L (2022) La casa como laboratorio: finanzas, vivienda y trabajo esencial. Consejo Latinoamericano de Ciencias Sociales, Buenos Aires
Galindo M (2013) No se puede descolonizar sin despatriarcalizar. Teoría y propuesta de la despatriarcalización. Mujeres Creando, La Paz
Gökarıksel B (2016) Intimate politics of protest: gendering embodiments and redefining spaces in Istanbul's Taksim Gezi Park and the Arab revolutions. In: Salime Z, Hasso FS (eds) Freedom without permission: bodies and space in the Arab revolutions. Duke University Press, Durham
Graeber D (2011) Debt: the first 5,000 years. Melville House, New York
Gudynas E (2009) Diez tesis urgentes sobre el nuevo extractivismo. http://www.rosalux.org.ec/pdfs/extractivismo.pdf#page=187. Accessed 10 November 2023
Harker C (2017) Debt space: topologies, ecologies and Ramallah, Palestine. Environ Plan D Soc Space 35(4):600–619
Harney S, Moten F (2013) The undercommons: fugitive planning and black study. Minor Compositions, New York
Harvey D (1982) The limits to capital. Basil Blackwell, Oxford
Harvey D (2011) L'enigma del capitale e il prezzo della sua sopravvivenza. Feltrinelli, Milano
Harvey D (2017) I movimenti non bastano per combattere il neoliberalismo. Interview to David Harvey. http://contropiano.org/news/politica-news/2017/07/20/movimenti-non-bastano-combattere-neoliberalismo-intervista-d-harvey-094123. Accessed 12 September 2023
Ho K (2015) Finance, anthropology of. In: International encyclopedia of the social & behavioral sciences. Elsevier, Amsterdam, pp 171–176
IMF (2017) Debt: glossary of selected financial terms. http://www.imf.org/external/np/exr/glossaryshowTerm.asp#93. Accessed 12 May 2023
Jabary-Salamanca O (2022) The stuff of life: frontier infrastructures of reproduction. Spotlight on racial capitalism. https://www.ijurr.org/spotlight-on/racial-capitalism/the-stuff-of-life-frontier-infrastructures-of-reproduction/. Accessed 21 July 2023
Jácome H (2005) Alcance de las microfinanzas en las ciudades de Quito, Guayaquil y Cuenca. In: Working paper, No. 05/201. FLACSO-Ecuador, Quito
Jácome H (2007) El sistema financiero y su papel en el desarrollo económico y social. In: La Tendencia. Revista de Análisis Político, No. 4, Quito
Jácome H, Cordovéz J (2004) Microfinanzas en la economía ecuatoriana: una alternativa para el desarrollo. FLACSO-Ecuador, Quito
Kast F, Pomeranz D (2014) Saving more to borrow less: experimental evidence from access to formal savings accounts in Chile. https://dash.harvard.edu/handle/1/11508214. Accessed 9 September 2023
Keiller P (2013) The view from the train. Cities and other landscapes. Verso, London
Kluender R, Mahoney N, Wong F, Yin W (2021) Medical debt in the US, 2009-2020. JAMA 326(3):250–256. https://www.ncbi.nlm.nih.gov/pmc/articles/PMC8293024/. Accessed 14 October 2022
Kluge A, Evans T, Liebman S (1990) The assault of the present on the rest of time. N German Crit 49:11–22
Larkin B (2013) The politics and poetics of infrastructure. Annu Rev Anthropol 42:327–343
Latour B (2020) Production or engendering? Foreword to Salmon: a red herring. https://www.e--flux.com/architecture/accumulation/345107/production-or-engendering/. Accessed 12 May 2022

Lazzarato M (2012) The making of the indebted man. MIT Press, Cambridge
Lazzarato M (2015) Governing by debt. Semiotext(e, Los Angeles
Lazzarato M, Alliez E (2021) Guerras y capital. Tinta Limón, Buenos Aires
LeBaron G (2014) Reconceptualizing debt bondage: debt as a class-based form of labor discipline. Crit Sociol 40(5):763–780
Lindblom C (1957) Still muddling, not yet through. Public Adm Rev 39:517–526
Lindblom C (1959) The science of 'muddling through'. Public Adm Rev 19:79–88
Luhmann N (1976) The future cannot begin: temporal structures in modern society. Soc Res 43(1):130–152
Mauss M (1954) The gift: the form and reason for exchange, archaic societies. Martino Fine Books, Eastford
McNamara R (1969) Address to the board of governors by Robert S. McNamara. Presidential speech. World Bank Group, Washington. http://documents.worldbank.org/curated/en/930801468315304694/Address-to-the-Board-of-Governors-by-Robert-S-McNamara. Accessed 2 December 2024
Meehan K, Strauss K (2015) Precarious worlds contested geographies of social reproduction. University of Georgia Press, Athens
Mezzadra S, Neilson B (2019) The politics of operations: excavating contemporary capitalism. Duke University Press, Durham
Mezzadri A (2019) On the value of social reproduction: informal labour, the majority world and the need for inclusive theories and politics. Radic Philos 204:33–41
Mideros A (2010) Crédito y desigualdad. Efecto del acceso a créditos en la brecha de ingreso de los hogares. FLACSO-Ecuador, Quito
Mies M (1986) Patriarchy and accumulation on a world scale. Zed Books, London
Mies M, Bennhold-Thomsen V (1999) The subsistence perspective: beyond the globalized economy. Zed Books, London
Milani C (2016) Il sovraindebitamento delle famiglie italiane. Welfare Oggi 4:54–57
Mitchell K, Marston SA, Katz C (2004) Life's work: an introduction, review and critique. In: Mitchell K, Marston SA, Katz C (eds) Life's work: geographies of social reproduction. Blackwell Publishing, Oxford, pp 1–26
Moore JW (2015) Ecologia-mondo e crisi del capitalismo. Ombre Corte, Verona
Morini C (2010) Per amore o per forza: femminilizzazione del lavoro e biopolitiche del corpo. Ombre Corte, Verona
Morton T, Boyer D (2021) Hyposubjects: on becoming human. Open Humanities Press, London
Mujeres Creando (2009) Mujeres Grafiteando. Compaz, La Paz
Murard L, Zylberman P (1976) Le Petit travailleur infatigable. Villes-usines, habitat et intimités au XIXe siecle. Recherches, Paris
Navarro M (2016) Despojo capitalista y luchas comunitarias en defensa de la vida México: claves desde la Ecología Política. ICSyH-BUAP, México
Patel R (2010) The value of nothing: how to reshape market society and redefine democracy. Picador, London
Patel R (2012) Stuffed and starved: the hidden battle for the world food system. Melville House, New York
Peck R, Miller J (2006) Future challenges in Latin American microfinance. In: Berger M, Goldmark L, Miller-Sanabria T (eds) An insider view of Latin American microfinance. Inter-American Development Bank, Washington
Peebles G (2010) The anthropology of credit and debt. Annu Rev Anthropol 39:225–240
Perulli P (2020) Il debito sovrano. La fase estrema del capitalismo. La nave di Teseo, Milano
Portes A, Hoffman K (2003) La estructura de clases en América Latina: composición y cambios durante la era neoliberal. Desarrollo Econ 43(171):355–387
Povinelli E (2011) Economies of abandonment. Duke University Press, Durham
Rama A (1984) La ciudad letrada. Ediciones del Norte, Hanover
Rolnik R (2018) Urban Warfare: Housing under the Empire of Finance. Verso, London
Rural Finance Network (2013) Boletín microfinanciero trimestral, No. 40, Quito. http://www.rfr.org. Accessed 12 August 2023

Rutland T (2010) The financialization of urban redevelopment. Geogr Compass 4(8):1167–1178
Sanguinetti P, Arreaza A, Rodríguez P, Álvarez F, Ortega D, Penfold M (2011) RED 2011: Servicios financieros para el desarrollo. Promoviendo el acceso en América Latina (Reporte de Economía y Desarrollo (RED). CAF, Caracas. https://scioteca.caf.com/handle/123456789/170. Accessed 6 June 2023
Schicks J (2013a) The definition and causes of microfinance over-indebtedness: a customer protection point of view. Oxf Dev Stud 41:95–116
Schicks J (2013b) The sacrifices of micro-borrowers in Ghana. A customer-protection perspective on measuring over-indebtedness. J Dev Stud 49:1238–1255
Schwarz J (2017) Platform logic: an interdisciplinary approach to the platform-based economy. Policy Internet 9:374–394
Sell R, Kunitz S (1986) The debt crisis and the end of an era in mortality decline. Stud Comp Int Dev 21(4):3–30
Shaw J (2020) Platform real estate: theory and practice of new urban real estate markets. Urban Geogr 41:8
Shorrocks A, Davies J, Lluberas R (2012) Credit Suisse Global wealth report 2012. Credit Suisse Research Institute, Zurich. https://publications.credit-suisse.com/tasks/render/file/index.cfm?fileid=88EE6EC8-83E8-EB92-9D5F39D5F5CD01F4. Accessed 3 May 2023
Simone A (2019) Contests over value: from the informal to the popular. Urban Stud 56(3):616–619
Sparke M, Sidaway JD, Bunnell T, Grundy-Warr C (2012) Geographies of Globalization. Routledge, London
Springer S (2016) The discourse of neoliberalism: an anatomy of a powerful idea. Rowman & Littlefield, Lanham
Stewart K (2007) Ordinary affects. Duke University Press, Durham
Stimilli E (2015) Debito e colpa. Ediesse, Roma
Superintendencia de Economía Popular y Solidaria (2013) Boletín Financiero. Sector Financiero Popular y Solidario al 30 de junio de 2013. http:// www.seps.gob.ec. Accessed 8 July 2023
Superintendencia de Economía Popular y Solidaria (2014) Ley orgánica de la economía popular y solidaria y del Sistema Financiero Popular y Solidario de 28 de abril de 2011, Quito. https://www.oas.org/juridico/pdfs/mesicic4_ecu_econ.pdf. Accessed 8 July 2023
UN-HABITAT (2003a) Slums of the world: the face of urban poverty in the new millennium? Earthscan, London. www.unhabitat.org/pmss/listItemDetails.aspx?publicationID=1124. Accessed 7 June 2022
UN-HABITAT (2003b) The challenge of slums: global report on human settlements 2003. Earthscan, London. www.unhabitat.org/pmss/listItemDetails.aspx?publication ID=1156. Accessed 25 June 2024
Vogelgesang U (2003) Microfinance in times of crisis: the effects of competition, rising indebtedness and economic crisis on repayment behavior. World Dev 31(12):2085–2114
Walter T, Wansleben L (2019), The assault of finance's 'present futures' on the rest of time. https://www.researchgate.net/publication337117890_The_assault_of_finance's_'present_futures'_on_the_rest_of_time. Accessed 23 April 2023
Weber R (2010) Selling city futures: the financialization of urban redevelopment policy. Econ Geogr 86(3):251–274
World Bank (2021) Robert S. McNamara at the World Bank, Retrospect. Development Reflections Series. World Bank, Washington
Zapata G (2013) The migration–development nexus: rendering migrants as transnational financial subjects through housing. Geoforum 47:93–102
Zibechi R (2012) Territories in resistance: cartography of Latin American social movements. AK Press, Baltimore

Debt and Economic-Cultural Resilience in Social Housing Programs in Quito: The Carapungo and Solanda Neighborhoods

Patricio Andino Sosa, David Pazmiño Amaya, and Rebeca Gallegos Bustamante

Abstract This study explores the economic and cultural resilience of social housing recipients in the Carapungo and Solanda neighborhoods of Quito, Ecuador. It examines the long-term impacts of housing debt, state intervention, and community organization on the livelihoods of residents. Through historical and qualitative analysis, the research highlights how debt functioned as both a stressor and a catalyst for social cohesion, community mobilization, and urban transformation. The findings suggest that residents developed survival strategies through collective action, informal savings mechanisms, and self-managed infrastructure improvements. Despite facing economic hardship and unfulfilled state promises, the residents of these neighborhoods demonstrated resilience by adapting their living spaces and strengthening community ties. However, contemporary challenges, such as insecurity and declining civic engagement, threaten the social fabric that once enabled collective resistance. The study contributes to discussions on urban development, debt, and resilience in the Global South.

Keywords Social housing · Economic resilience · Debt and urban development · Community self-management

---

P. Andino Sosa (✉) · D. Pazmiño Amaya
International University of Ecuador (UIDE), Business School, Quito, Ecuador
e-mail: edandinoso@uide.edu.ec; dapazminoam@uide.edu.ec

R. Gallegos Bustamante
Faculty of Arts, Design and Architecture, International University of Ecuador (UIDE), Quito, Ecuador
e-mail: egallegosbu@uide.edu.ec

A. di Campli (ed.), *Inhabiting Debt*, The Latin American Studies Book Series,
https://doi.org/10.1007/978-3-031-99886-7_2

1 Background

Homeownership is a major life goal for most individuals and families, as it represents not only a place to live but also a symbol of stability, investment, and personal growth. It is of paramount importance because it intertwines financial security with a sense of achievement and long-term well-being. While the aspiration to own a home is present across all socio-economic groups, it becomes even more significant in popular sectors, where economic hardship, political instability, and cultural barriers make access to housing particularly challenging. For these communities, obtaining their own home is not just a milestone but a fundamental step toward improving their quality of life and securing a better future.

As a country's economic development increases, the quality of life of its inhabitants also tends to improve, particularly in terms of broader and more accessible opportunities for obtaining adequate housing. This hypothesis was explored in the Ecuadorian context, focusing on the social housing programs implemented during the 1970s and 1980s in the neighborhoods of Carapungo and Solanda in Quito.[1] The central premise of this study was to examine the economic and cultural experiences—both individual and collective—that took shape throughout the processes of housing allocation, indebtedness, repayment, and expansion. To carry out this research, we engaged with the founding residents who continue to live in these neighborhoods and who were directly involved in the aforementioned processes, allowing us to gain first-hand insight into their trajectories and challenges.[2] Respondents fell into the socio-economic strata C+ and C−.[3] Data collection took

---

[1] Research carried out in 2023 by the Faculties of Architecture and the Business School of the International University of Ecuador, in collaboration with the Politecnico di Torino.

[2] The profile of the interviewees in the two neighborhoods consisted mainly of elderly individuals, mostly retired, with some still engaged in retail aspects of their business. At the time of the interview, these individuals belonged to socio-economic groups C+ and C−.

[3] In Ecuador, the classification of socioeconomic groups is based on criteria related to income, education level, type of employment, and other well-being indicators. C+: This stratum represents the lower-middle segment of the middle class. It includes families with moderate incomes, often with secondary or higher education, formal employment, and access to essential goods and services. They have a certain level of economic stability but may be vulnerable to economic crises. C−: This group is on the border between the lower middle class and the popular sectors. It includes individuals with more precarious incomes, often engaged in informal or less-stable employment. They have limited access to goods and services compared to the C+ group but are not in conditions of extreme poverty. These categories are used for market studies, socioeconomic analysis, and public policy design to better understand the social structure and consumption dynamics in Ecuador. The socioeconomic stratification survey conducted in 2011 by El Instituto Nacional de Estadísticas y Censos (the National Institute of Statistics and Census) presented the following groups with the percentages of the population belonging to each group: A (1.9%); B (11.2%); C+ (22.8%); C− (49.3%); D (14.9%). The strata are created by the sum of points obtained from the following socioeconomic variables: housing, goods, technology, economy, mail and social networks, consumption habits, and level of schooling. Each stratum is defined by the following number of points: stratum A from 845 to 1000; stratum B from 696 to 845; stratum C+ from 535 to 696; stratum C− from 316 to 535; and stratum D from 0 to 316 (Borja-Nuñez 2011).

place in the first half of the year 2023. The questionnaire was designed according to the established categories of analysis and the selection of respondents was done by purposive or criterion sampling, participants were those who met certain characteristics relevant to the research.

To better understand the conditions that shaped the development of social housing plans, it is important to consider that Quito's urban expansion became significantly more dynamic in the second half of the twentieth century, driven by economic growth, particularly the rise of agricultural exports. At the time, the city was still characterized by working-class neighborhoods and peripheral haciendas. Meanwhile, the country was undergoing extreme political instability, which ultimately led to the establishment of a military dictatorship.[4] During this government, several measures were ratified to promote greater participation of the country in international markets; one such measure was Ecuador's participation in LAFTA, the Latin American Free Trade Association (Martínez-Molina 2007).[5] The city's economic development led to a growth in the population; this brought with it a need for housing, mass transport, public recreation spaces, and other services; these demands later increased due to the country's oil boom. As a result, the economy triggered the creation of socio-economic spaces in the city: "The preference for living in the North continued, leaving the North differentiated with wealthy families, and the South, with a population of restricted economy. In the historic centre, on the other hand, slums appeared" (Martínez-Molina 2007, p. 15).[6]

Two spaces existed in the urban environment at the end of the 1970s and 1980s: one at the northern end (Carapungo), and the other at the southern end (Solanda); these areas served as settlements for social housing plans. Previously, the Solanda and Carapungo neighborhoods were large agricultural estates and cattle ranches which, given the city's geographical characteristics and notable longitudinal growth, provided a sufficient number of lots for social housing plans.[7] The Solanda neighborhood, located in the southern part of Quito, attracted internal migration in the 1970s; it consolidated its identity thanks to the varied and diverse cultural influences of its first inhabitants. Conversely, Carapungo, located in the northern part of the city, had been occupied by indigenous populations since pre-Columbian times. Like Solanda, its internal migrants were peasants and families from several popular sectors of the city, creating a fertile cultural space enriched by Afro-Ecuadorians.

When the founding inhabitants of Solanda and Carapungo acquired their debt to purchase social housing, their occupations included, among others: teachers in

---

[4] The dictatorship was formed by officers Ramón Castro Jijón, Marcos Gándara Enríquez, Luis Cabrera Sevilla, and Guillermo Freile Posso. They ruled from July 1963 to March 1966.

[5] A regional economic integration agency that existed between 1960 and 1980 later became ALADI, Asociación Latinoamericana de Integración.

[6] Original text: *Continuaba la preferencia por vivir en el Norte quedando totalmente diferenciado el Norte con familias pudientes, y el Sur, con población de economía restringida. En el Centro histórico, en cambio, aparecieron los tugurio*s. Translated by the authors

[7] In the 1980s, the longitudinal physical growth model became prevalent. This spatial model, developed in 1950, remained in use until 1990 (Zhingre 2020).

public and private schools, domestic servants, micro-entrepreneurs, low-ranking public servants, employees of private companies, and independent traders. The initial inhabitants of these neighborhoods shared homogeneous cultural roots (ideas, values, and customs) as well as common goals and challenges, namely, the need to have their own homes.

2 Debt and Resilience

Analyzing economic and cultural resilience is particularly interesting to understand the experiences and education of individuals and social groups that, for several years, have had to deal with stressful events associated with the process of debt repayment under the acquisition of social housing in the neighborhoods of Solanda and Carapungo in the city of Quito.

Resilience is a term that has emerged and gained importance in recent decades. Its increased influence is due to its application in various fields of knowledge, including physics, health, education, sociology, ecology, and economics. Given its wide application, it is difficult to structure a universal concept of resilience (Becoña 2006; Cabanyes Truffino 2010). For this study, we will use definitions closest to those of social sciences, where resilience is associated with the adaptive human capacity (individual or group) to handle adverse situations and positively overcome one or more stressful phenomena within a dynamic, elastic, and variable process, depending on how much volatility, temporality, and spatiality was influenced by the stressor (Becoña 2006; Kotliarenco et al. 1997; Tapia 2012).

In social practice, personal adversities (death of family or friends, family conflicts, debts, drug abuse, gender violence, poverty, mental health) and collective adversities (wars, chronic exposure to violence, epidemics, deportations, economic conflicts, migrations) catalyze processes that expose individuals or collectives to a stress load; the latter will vary according to the impact and importance of the stressor phenomenon that catalyzed the adversities (Tapia 2012; Uriarte Arciniega 2013).

Latin America and, in general, the global south, are territories constantly characterized by conflicts that vary in intensity and duration. These adversities arise from cultural, economic, and political clashes, due to both internal and external influences. The cultural identity of these peoples is violated by actions of colonization, denial, subjugation, exclusion, marginalization, and poverty (Quintero 2018). Since Latin Americans have had to endure these difficult conditions, they have developed practices to overcome these conflicts, such as forms of self-protection mediated by cognitive, subjective, and organizational processes (Lopez Bracamonte and Limón Aguirre 2016). In this scenario, attachment to their territories and common traditions is of significant importance (Becoña 2006; Cabanyes Truffino 2010).

Taking on economic debt becomes a significant stressor for individuals or communities. The initial concept of debt involves a person or institution owning something of economic value and lending it to another person or institution in the hope of obtaining an additional benefit, based on the trust that future repayment is guaranteed. This brief description encompasses philosophical ideas and economic approaches that are not new. They are inspired either by Socratic virtue—debt is a concept linked to duty and divine power—or by Hume's concepts regarding the need to tackle the economic dynamics of Ecuador, which has historically experienced numerous stressors that have affected its population in many ways. In the 1970s, a period close to the one in question, the decline in the prices of raw materials (e.g., cocoa and coffee) on world markets had negative effects on Ecuador's economy, worsening the situation in the country and, in particular, affecting the less affluent population, which expressed its discontent through strikes and social protests (CEPAL 2023; Paz and Miño Cepeda 1994).[8]

Between 1964 and 1973, Ecuador experienced a trade deficit due to a decrease in banana exports and an increase in imports. In 1972, the start of state oil exports marked a turning point for the country; its entry into the international hydrocarbon markets significantly revived the economy, resulting in an "oil bonanza" that boosted industrialization and both public and private investments. In the 1970s and 1980s, Ecuador adopted a policy known as ISI, "Industrialización por sustitución de importaciones" or "Industrialization by Import Substitution," aimed at promoting the growth of its national industry. During this positive period, Ecuador accessed greater credit, which led to an increase in external public debt and a growth in imports (Acosta 2006; Martín-Mayoral 2009).

The increased economic flows from the oil boom led to several social transformations, including population growth in large cities and increased urbanization in popular areas. Urban groups related to industry, commerce, and the financial sector became more dynamic, especially in Guayaquil and Quito, where most of the oil investment was concentrated. As a result, these cities became attractive hubs for internal migration from the countryside (Paz and Miño Cepeda 1994). However, the growth in public wealth also triggered social discontent, revealing social and regional inequalities.

The crisis in Ecuador in the 1980s was caused by a drop in international oil prices, leading to a reduction in fiscal revenues and a subsequent decrease in investments in infrastructure and public services. This resulted in an economic recession and a decline in the quality of life in both urban and rural areas; unemployment increased, especially in the industrial sector. The growing wave of rural-to-urban migration put pressure on housing, health, and education services. The unstable political and economic landscape at the time hindered the implementation of effective public policies to address social problems, preventing adequate responses to new and challenging urban issues (Acosta 2006).

---

[8] A proposal that sought to develop national industry by preventing imports of manufactured goods. It was proposed around 1950 by the Economic Commission for Latin America (CEPAL) under the leadership of Zhingre (2020).

3 The Seduction of the "Home of One's Own"

When León Febres Cordero became President of Ecuador, he based his policies on neoliberal guidelines, aiming for increased private sector participation and minimal state involvement. During his electoral campaign, he promised to reduce the housing deficit and improve living conditions through subsidies and soft credits for housing acquisition.[9] The focus was on vulnerable sectors of society, which led to challenges in urban planning and development, particularly in the appropriation and use of land (Rodriguez 1989).

Contrary to Febres Cordero's initial premises, the public sector was directly involved in social housing projects through the Banco Ecuatoriano de la Vivienda (BEV) and funding from the United States Agency for International Development (USAID).[10] The construction of low-income housing projects was boosted through the financing of offers from state institutions, mutual savings, and credit cooperatives (Van Sluys and Jaramillo 2021). State intervention played a fundamental role by creating the Junta Nacional de la Vivienda (JNV), an institution which, together with the BEV and the Instituto Ecuatoriano de Seguridad Social (IESS), financed 66.7% of the housing built in the country during that period (del Aguirre 1980).[11]

For Oquendo, the changes in the country's socio-economic conditions in the 1970s and 1980s were the spark leading to the emergence of new social agents that reconfigured the city's urban structure (Oquendo 1986). Urban development in Quito is on the rise, according to Ponce and Valencia (1981), quoted by Oquendo: "Quito had a constant growth rate of around 4% until 1974 and accelerated its growth between 1974 and 1977 when it grew at a rate of 5.78%" (Oquendo 1986, p. 68).[12]

It is in this context of economic growth and new social actors that social housing plans emerged in Quito in Solanda and Carapungo, the so-called "children of the oil boom" neighborhoods that had been built to help reduce the urban housing deficit caused by population growth and internal migration. The sizeable land area of these neighborhoods guaranteed massive housing construction. By 1982 the National Census reported that 30.5% of Quito's housing was inadequate; it also reported problems regarding basic services and overcrowding. Only 24% of the dwellings had a combined use of brick, concrete, or block (Dudley 1986).

---

[9] León Febres Cordero's presidential term ran from 1984 to 1988.

[10] This authority was created in 1961 with initial financing composed of 66% foreign capital while the remaining 34% was national (IESS and the National Government). The support and protection given by the state to mutualism were fundamental for its development (...) it served to channel international loans toward mutualism and private banking (Carrión 1986, p. 113).

[11] The JNV was created in February 1974.

[12] Original text: *Quito tiene un ritmo de crecimiento constante de alrededor del 4% hasta 1974 y acelera su crecimiento entre 1974 y 1977 en que crece a un ritmo de 5 0.78%*. Translated by the authors.

The social housing programs had a preestablished structure, based on the traditional models established by the World Bank, Dudley reminds us of the composition of the housing proposed in the 1970s and 1980s in Ecuador, namely:

> Very small houses made in the manner seen in the illusion of plastered block or brick, with a reinforced concrete or steel structure, and with all services. A 21 m^2 house like the basic ones of the "Plan Techo" has a price for bathroom and toilet facilities almost the same as a 100 m^2 house (Dudley 1986, p. 36).[13]

Similarly, Carrión (1986) describes the conditions of the "unidades basicas" or "basic units"—the name used for social housing—giving us a clear idea of the space that the families would occupy.[14] In the minds of the future inhabitants of the social housing plans, the houses they would occupy had adequate structural engineering to support extensions and the possibility of adding additional floors. This potential acted like a magnet, igniting the hopes and dreams of these sectors of the population. They envisioned the possibility of making their investment profitable and securing future housing options for their children or other family members. The prospect of having a home that could grow with their needs provided a sense of stability and long-term planning, fostering a greater sense of community and optimism for the future. Additionally, the ability to customize and expand their homes allowed families to adapt to changing circumstances and requirements over time, enhancing their overall quality of life and contributing to a stronger, more resilient community.

3.1 The Lie with an Official Face

It was very hard for the inhabitants of Carapungo and Solanda to try and buy their homes during the difficult political and economic conditions that existed in the country. The first major obstacle for citizens to overcome was raising the money required for the "enganche" or reservation of the housing quota. For those who managed to reserve their housing, another extremely complex stress factor emerged when the BEV and the JNV handed over the houses. The situation was very disturbing: the initial proposal illustrated in models and plans turned out to be completely different; they received a half-built, incomplete house based on the concept of a

[13] Original text: *Casas muy pequeñas hechas de la manera vista en la ilusión de bloque o ladrillo enlucido, con estructura de hormigón armado o acero, y con todos los servicios. Una casa de 21 metros cuadrados como los básicos del "Plan Techo" tiene un precio para el baño y las instalaciones de los servicios casi lo mismo como una casa de 100 metros cuadrados* (Oquendo 1986, p. 36). Translated by the authors.

[14] The "Basic Unit" consists of an initial room of 21 m^2 with a separate toilet. It serves as a nucleus that can be expanded according to the needs and possibilities of the interested parties, in line with the alternative designs envisioned for this purpose by the JNV. Its maximum price is the equivalent of 42 minimum wages (the minimum monthly remuneration received by a worker in Ecuador) (Carrión 1986, p. 113).

"flat-roof" construction. In addition, in both cases, there were serious, multiple deficiencies in the basic services of electricity, drinking water, roads, and communal spaces.

The two housing plans taken into consideration did not have adequate road infrastructure, causing serious mobility and security problems. Neither did they have basic electricity, water, or telephone services, again causing numerous problems for the inhabitants; paradoxically, the inhabitants had to pay for public services without receiving them.[15] The general feeling of the interviewees, when they recalled these events, is one of annoyance at the disrespect experienced by people who longed for their own homes; they described the initial housing offer that never materialized as a hoax. They felt that the real conditions in which the inhabitants of these neighborhoods would live never really mattered, that political action took precedence, inspired by the narrative delivered by politicians that "they were doing construction work." There was a feeling that the state did not mind lying and subjecting low-income families to a poor quality of life. They pointed out that the first stages during which they acquired their homes were dramatic and plagued with individual and community problems; nevertheless, they persisted in solving the problems and improving their living conditions.

Despite these challenges, the residents of Carapungo and Solanda demonstrated remarkable resilience and determination. They organized themselves into community groups to address the deficiencies in their neighborhoods, working together to improve infrastructure and access to basic services. Over time, their collective efforts led to significant improvements in their living conditions, fostering a sense of solidarity and shared purpose among the inhabitants. This experience not only highlighted the shortcomings of the initial housing plans but also underscored the strength and resourcefulness of the communities in overcoming adversity. Their persistence in facing these issues head-on and their ability to collaborate as a community were crucial in transforming their neighborhoods into more livable and thriving environments.

This journey was not just about building houses but creating a sense of belonging and community. The shared hardships and collective efforts to overcome them forged strong bonds among the residents. They became a living testament to the power of community spirit and mutual support, proving that even in the face of significant challenges, solidarity and resilience can lead to meaningful progress and improved quality of life.

[15] Such was the case of the payment for drinking water in Carapungo; after some time, the inhabitants discovered they were receiving well water.

3.2 Resilience, Revolts, and Community Self-Management

The initial, serious problems regarding the quality of the housing provided and lack of basic services led to the first collective mobilizations organized to solve the issues. Lopez Bracamonte and Limón Aguirre (2016) argue that, when organizing collective struggles, socio-political components are generated during formal and informal negotiations within the community and when dealing with different approaches to public institutions. Permanent action during the struggles undertaken by the residents of the neighborhoods in question triggered an increase in formal and informal community participation. This led to the establishment of permanent and democratic channels of communication, as well as a sense of commitment and cultural identity (values, beliefs, and customs) shared and recognized as their own by each neighborhood. From the outset, the residents of Carapungo and Solanda saw themselves as key community actors, and in the thick of the actions undertaken, they built a sense of belonging and solidarity with an increase in collective self-esteem, generating what Borja-Nuñez (2011) called a "moral corpus."

It is important to highlight the remarkable intervention of women in the development of urban community organizations, occupying spaces that men had traditionally managed. Women's leadership was experienced in two ways: one as "housewives" and the other as "neighborhood leaders." In the first case, they consolidated their role as the unifying force of the family nucleus, while in the second, they decisively broke through cultural assumptions that made their participation invisible and relegated it to the background. It is crucial to note that the leadership positions occupied by women were obtained democratically through votes by neighborhood residents, as seen in Carapungo.

Thanks to their organization, social agitation, and presence in the streets, the women's groups were very influential and experienced in the struggles they undertook, especially in developing cooperation mechanisms among neighbors.

Another noteworthy aspect is that when the neighborhood organizations were first formed, the atmosphere was influenced by several political parties. The large population in the social housing estates was fiercely sought after by political parties that considered Solanda and Carapungo as fertile ground for the emergence of local leaders to serve as links, given that traditional political parties were managed in a caudillista and patriarchal manner (Borja-Nuñez 2011).

The numerous, complex social problems faced by the inhabitants of Carapungo and Solanda led to practices and knowledge that emerged during their most intensive cultural actions. This knowledge was nourished by their historical memory—both as individuals and as a group—and their strong, enduring relationship with their territories. On one hand, Solanda's identity was shaped by internal migration from popular sectors, while on the other, Carapungo had a broader cultural palette, including internal migrants and people from indigenous and Afro-Ecuadorian sectors. The abilities and skills developed by these communities allowed them to overcome adverse events and achieve certain breakthroughs, framed in what Alzugaray called "collective efficacy" (Lopez Bracamonte and Limón Aguirre 2016).

This idea is illustrated by the struggle to eliminate the UVC ("Unidad de Valor Constante" or the Constant Value Unit), a process that energized neighborhood organization and community participation, thus consolidating a more cohesive and militant neighborhood structure. The population of Carapungo led the fight to eliminate the UVC in Quito and later nationally.[16]

Community organization and participation rocketed sky-high in the two neighborhoods, making it possible for the communities to independently self-manage their problems, even without the participation of other municipal and governmental authorities. Proclaiming community self-organizations was enough to kindle the enthusiastic collaboration of neighbors. This is how they were able, for example, to solve the lack of schools and transportation. It is interesting to note that this kind of neighborhood organization spread to adjacent districts with similar problems.

3.3 *The Long Road of Debt: Survival Strategies*

It is worth emphasizing that when the debt was incurred, the neighborhood consisted of newly formed family structures, mostly young married couples with infant children. The debt burden was borne equally by both spouses. Payments were made depending on the employment situation of each partner; however, there were also cases where single or divorced individuals, who had longed for several years to have a "little house of their own"—a concept that the political narrative later transformed into "decent housing"—made payments.

In the initial critical moments of dealing with family debt, women played a key role in the two neighborhoods because most of them managed the family's economy and were directly responsible for payments to the lending institutions. Sometimes they even assumed direct payment as the sole contributors. In any case, women were the "face" visible to the financial institutions and control authorities.

Funding to purchase social housing units came from various sources, including state loans, private savings, family loans, business loans, and additional working hours. The most common debt repayment method involved monthly installments over several years. The original debts to state institutions had different repayment terms; many were paid off before the established deadlines. The dollarization process in Ecuador benefited several debtors, allowing them to repay their debts in shorter periods than initially agreed. In other cases, monthly installments were

[16] "The 'Unidad de Valor Constante' (UVC) or the Constant Value Unit (CVU) is a measure that maintains the real value of the currency and is periodically readjusted according to the increase in the general price level. The UVC is an instrument designed to encourage long-term financing of assets (...) facilitating the financing of housing" (Suárez-Giordano 1994, p. 165). The progressive monthly payments that respondents had to make for the application of the UVC were initially 600 sucres, which then rose to 900 sucres.

significantly reduced when they exchanged sucres for dollars.[17] Nevertheless, the initial stage of Ecuadorian dollarization was traumatic for many Ecuadorians who either lost the savings they had managed to accumulate or saw a sharp fall in their capital when converting sucres into dollars. This led to one of the country's most traumatic emigration processes, primarily to Europe and the United States.

The debt significantly impacted the family budgets of most interviewees, sometimes reaching as high as 50%. This situation forced inhabitants to either request advance payments from their employers or look for additional jobs to balance their finances. There were also several instances of late payment of monthly instalments, compelling citizens to engage in multiple activities to generate extra income.

It was impossible to obtain reliable documentation indicating the total amount of debt owed by the inhabitants of Carapungo and Solanda. After 30 years of debt, the residents did not clearly remember the payment conditions, final amounts, or the duration of their indebtedness. In several cases, they took out additional loans to repay the original debt, resulting in new debt.

During the initial debt process, the main lender was the Banco Ecuatoriano de la Vivienda, a state bank that later continued to grant loans for housing extensions, which many people accessed. This process was complicated by the application of credit in UVC, with fluctuating interest and capital, causing many problems for those in debt.

3.4 Building the Family's Future

Over time, the original space of the dwellings became insufficient for the growing number of family members, necessitating extensions to address the problem. There were other reasons as well, such as improving the house's aesthetics and the need for more social spaces. Additionally, from the moment they moved into their houses, the inhabitants had the idea of enlarging them to be used in the future by their closest family members (children, grandchildren), thus ensuring them a home of their own.

Many inhabitants in Carapungo and Solanda enlarged or modified their original houses; a house with its original design, i.e., exactly as it was when initially delivered, was very rare. The extensions far exceeded the square meters initially purchased; in many cases, the houses were built up to three stories. The inhabitants mentioned that they did not hire architects or engineers for these works; instead, the construction was carried out by masons they knew personally. They also failed to regularize the extensions or alterations with the Municipality of Quito, thus exponentially increasing the illegal status of this type of construction. To undertake the extensions or alterations, new debt was incurred from various sources, including

[17] In 2000, the Ecuadorian economy was dollarized. The exchange rate went from 25,000 sucres to one dollar.

private financial institutions, inter-family loans, loans from the Ecuadorian Institute of Social Security (IESS), inhabitants' savings, and the sale of family assets. Interestingly, a savings system was developed by the inhabitants of the two neighborhoods. This "family self-savings" system involved setting aside small amounts of money on a fortnightly or monthly basis until the planned amounts were accrued, enabling small or medium-sized works to be carried out in the houses. This system was applied over various periods, sometimes even months, depending on the scope of the work required. Short periods were used to save what was necessary to install a door or plaster a few walls, while longer periods were needed to build walls or cast slabs. This explains why the extensions were so slow to be implemented, often taking several years to complete. In many cases, children contributed to the family savings once they grew up and started working, leading to improved economic conditions for several families and greater progress in the works.

Although the financial resources for the extensions varied, they were insufficient. As a result, mechanisms were established to maximize the profitability of the capital obtained, especially concerning hired labor. In several cases, the inhabitants themselves hired this kind of labor; they were responsible for the works either individually or together with family and friends, recalling an ancestral pre-Columbian practice of community collaboration called "Minga".[18]

For most families, the decision to extend their dwellings involved economic sacrifices that varied from small to substantial. In some cases, this even meant depriving themselves of food, going for walks, or addressing health problems—all of which impacted the quality of family life. While it is true that becoming indebted to purchase a house or implement extensions and improvements involved enormous sacrifices, by the time of the interviews, all the people had paid off not only their original debts but also most of their debts for the extensions or alterations to their houses. Different criteria came into play when considering the possibility of acquiring new debt for home improvements: some were willing to continue becoming indebted, but most had no plans to incur new debts. By fully repaying the original debt, the residents experienced feelings of peace of mind and ownership of the property they had acquired. Having something of their own and not having to pay rent was mentioned as the main benefit. The feeling of owning one's own home was, at this point, considered an important family incentive; it also consolidated the profitability of the initial investment. This sense of stability and security contributed to a better quality of life and provided a foundation for future generations.

While there was a sense of peace of mind at the end of the debt repayment, the interviewees recalled the great personal and family sacrifices they had to make, especially during the first years of repayment. They associated the process of debt repayment with a fatal and inescapable destiny that had to be assumed by popular sectors to obtain housing. The experience of overcoming financial hardship and ultimately achieving homeownership became a source of pride and resilience for

[18] See di Campli in this book, page 32.

many families, illustrating their determination and perseverance in the face of adversity.

3.5 *Two Strangers: The Past and the Present*

The interviewees who still lived in Carapungo and Solanda mentioned that living in their neighborhoods is now dangerous due to the increase in street vending and the arrival of foreign migrants; according to them, this has led to problems of insecurity and higher levels of violence. They indicated that one of the main problems is the poor police protection they receive and the low level of community organization they currently have. The new neighbors are indifferent to the current problems of the neighborhood; they mention that the newly-arrived residents are more individualistic and do not seek to work toward a common good, causing permanent differing visions and discrepancies between old and new neighbors.

They also mentioned the lack of governmental support, especially from the Municipality of Quito, which does not provide adequate nighttime lighting in the neighborhoods. While the parks have helped develop recreational activities for the inhabitants, problems are evident in the ravines. The current relationship between neighbors from different sectors of the neighborhood is marked by a series of intercultural conflicts. These conflicts are due to racial differences, the coexistence of different nationalities, and economic, political, and idiosyncratic differences. The serious nature of these problems is exacerbated in Carapungo by the number of inhabitants and the diverse composition of the different kinds of individuals living in the neighborhood.

A significant cultural difference is evident in the community practices of the "old" neighbors versus the "new" neighbors. Most of the new neighbors are referred to as the "other groups"; the old neighbors try to ignore these groups because, according to them, when the new inhabitants began to buy or rent houses, they altered the social relations that had existed for years in the neighborhoods. The old neighbors believe this has changed the social and cultural composition that had existed for several years. They also stated that it was difficult to coexist with neighbors of other nationalities, especially Venezuelans, who are numerous and express themselves according to their customs and habits. Foreigners, and individuals from poor or excluded sectors, are associated with the current levels of delinquency, particularly assaults, robberies, and drug dealing.

In Carapungo, problems also exist with neighbors from rural, indigenous, and black populations who are identified as people who "have other customs." Socialization between neighbors from the same neighborhoods who live in different sectors and face specific problems is also problematic. The interviewees expressed concern and nostalgia for the loss of strong community participation. They nostalgically and emphatically mentioned the initial processes of neighborhood organization, which they considered a unifying element that effectively resolved community problems. There is a persistent yearning to return to old social practices such as collective decision-making, popular assemblies, and other formal and informal mechanisms that had strong support, authority, and efficiency in uniting the voices of the communities.

4 Final Reflections

Given the new economic conditions in the 1970s and 1980s, Quito experienced significant urban expansion with the presence of new social actors who demanded more and better housing options. This situation mobilized state entities (BEV, JNV, IESS) to intervene in the planning, construction, and financing of social housing plans. However, the state proposal implemented by the central government failed to respond efficiently to the demands of emerging sectors in the city. The delivery of the "piso-techo" or "flat-roof" housing type disrespected the hopes and dignity of future inhabitants by providing them with incomplete houses lacking basic services.

At the beginning of this document, we hypothesized that an improvement in a country's economic development leads to an enhancement in the quality of life for its inhabitants, especially when they have more opportunities to obtain housing. The information collected in the Solanda and Carapungo neighborhoods partially supports this assumption. While housing was indeed obtained, the quality of life during the debt repayment process was traumatic for most families, who had to rely on cultural and economic resilience mechanisms to achieve their goals.

The stories about the socially stressful issues experienced by inhabitants of social housing projects in Quito suggest that people can build cultural and economic resilience, even in complex conditions where state agencies fail to fulfill their basic responsibilities in terms of infrastructure, services, and security. The study of cultural resilience processes made it possible to record participatory democratic activities and the emergence of collective leadership with strong similarities in the two neighborhoods. These situations of collective struggle triggered community participation, rooted in bonds of identity that the residents of the neighborhoods turned into efficient actions to solve their common problems and thus ensure that they overcame the adversities they had to deal with. One notable aspect was the role played by women's collectives in creating networks of support and struggle, as well as acting as the leaders of general processes of organization, meeting, and social cohesion.

The communities in question were able to cope resiliently with the stressors that put their normal social development at risk. It was uncomfortable for residents and their families to have to endure a situation that lasted for 20–30 years, under initial conditions that were very adverse for survival and with long-term debt. They could move forward thanks to a combination of cultural knowledge, social skills, and community organizational strategies. Neighborhood organization and the exploitation of cultural heritage promoted coherent combative actions that were key to overcoming the neighborhoods' initial problems; in turn, this led to obtaining, and later improving, the quality of public services and the consolidation of collective leadership. It was noted that in the reality of neighborhood social practice, while communities struggled and resisted, their accrued knowledge guided their actions, bestowing meaning on the practical behavior of community resistance, for example, when they faced the initial problems of being given their homes with serious infrastructure deficiencies and lack of public services, in addition to their commitment to having to pay the debt—all this in the midst of the economic, political, and social turbulence that gripped Ecuador in the 1970s and 1980s.

During the analysis of the economic and cultural resilience processes, elements were detected based on beliefs and motivations to achieve long-term goals, within the framework of an adequate management of social, political, and economic pressure. The analysis identified community resilience skills used to provide support in the face of stressful processes; the core element of these actions was always their reciprocal bond of support; they always felt and saw themselves as a community marked by beliefs and values practically solved by exploiting a common cultural matrix.

The alterations and extensions made to the houses were managed to leave habitable spaces for children and grandchildren; this inheritance built in the present demanded the crucial participation of the beneficiaries (children, grandchildren). The long road to repayment of the housing debt had a double meaning: from an initial moment of "enduring misfortune" to a second moment of "growing stronger through misfortune and growing up." In the end, residents were able to pay off their initial housing debts but felt that they had to experience considerable family sacrifices in the process.

The community participation that was the decisive matrix for solving the initial problems of the neighborhoods weakened at the end of the twentieth century. This undermined the sense of belonging and the common significance created by neighborhood social practices. There were several attempts to revive community and cultural aspects, but these were on a small scale and with little collective impact. At present, the neighborhoods in question do not have the same level of organization and leadership they did 30 years ago. The new generations and the new neighbors have not had the capacity or motivation to generate collective leadership with the ability to fight; instead, they reflect "social apathy." Despite the current difficult and contradictory living conditions in these communities, the interviewees have not abandoned their homes; on the contrary, they show great affection and a sense of belonging toward their neighborhoods. Indeed, Solanda shows signs of reactivating community organization due to the current problem endured by several houses that underwent structural alterations after the construction of the city's subway system; however, this has not led to the emergence of new leadership and forms of organization.

For the inhabitants of Carapungo and Solanda, taking on long-term debt involved generating a mechanism of struggle and economic resistance, framed within the concept of "living within and against" proposed by Aníbal Quijano, where the option of life becomes a subversive act in the face of the global domination patterns of the modern/capitalist world-system. In these social scenarios of social housing debt in Quito, the interrelated triad of domination, exploitation, and conflict was used to control the "resources" of the main spheres of social existence: work, subjectivity, and collective authority (Palermo 2009; Quijano 2014; Assis Clímaco 2020).

This economic resistance was not only a survival mechanism but also a form of defiance against the inequities imposed by the larger socioeconomic system. By enduring the long-term debt, the residents actively resisted the forces that sought to marginalize them. They leveraged their cultural knowledge and community ties to navigate these challenges, demonstrating remarkable resilience and solidarity. Through collective efforts and shared struggles, they managed to create spaces of autonomy and agency within a system designed to oppress.

The persistence of the severe conditions of debt and harsh initial living conditions of the inhabitants of social housing also produced collective epistemic alternatives that tackled the intention of those in power to alter intersubjectivity and present the inhabitants of the neighborhoods in question as "modern" and "civilized"—ignoring their rich, diverse cultural heritage. In Solanda and Carapungo, many voices, experiences, and beliefs were amalgamated to draft an epistemic proposal; the social struggles of the neighborhoods acted as a melting pot, merging many cultural expressions, very similar to an "Ecology of Knowledge" (de Santos 2009, 2010). This knowledge emerged from popular sites and levels of collective resistance, rooted in community practices, and from other types of knowledge not necessarily scientific or Western Eurocentric. The experiences, knowledge, and cultural practices of the popular neighborhoods allowed them to struggle against the neoliberal proposal emanating from the prevailing Ecuadorian state.

The inhabitants who were consulted expressed their general vision of the debt repayment process, considering it as a "fatality of the future," where pain, sacrifice, and hope coexisted in order to achieve their great dream—home ownership. The strong influence of neoliberal policies in the social housing programs of the 1980s in Quito was intended to produce a unique and unquestionable state narrative: market proposals and practices were inevitable since they were the only available life options; they were the only option to achieve "social development," "to be modern," and to be able to live as "civilized people." The state narrative created a space to culturally and ethically legitimize debt processes.

The struggle by the community became a phenomenon of economic and cultural resilience toward their debt; it has an ontological similarity to the life experiences of the Colombian Caribbean fishermen of the Grande de La Magdalena river, studied by Fals Borda (2002) and summarized in the concept of the "Hombre-hicotea" and "Sentipensante." These concepts embody the integration of feeling and thinking, highlighting how the residents of Carapungo and Solanda navigated their challenges with a blend of emotional intelligence and practical wisdom. This approach allowed them to develop innovative strategies to cope with their financial burdens while preserving their cultural identity and fostering a strong sense of community solidarity:

> The "Hombre-hicotea" who knows how to be enduring in order to face the setbacks of life and be able to overcome them, who, in adversity, encloses himself and then returns to existence with the same energy as before, is also the thinking man who combines reason and

> love, body and heart, to get rid of all the (bad) formations that dismember this harmony and to be able to speak the truth.
> (Moncayo 2015, p. 10).

The people who undertook debt repayment processes for several years to acquire social housing in Quito created a life practice that closely aligns with the philosophy of life proposed by Fals Borda and the social practices performed from the perspective of economic and cultural resilience.[19] The strategies they implemented allowed them to overcome, with dignity and patience, the setbacks that occurred during the payment process. Individually and collectively, they watched over the future of their families and their neighborhoods.

Competing Interest The authors of this chapter declare that they have no financial, institutional, or personal conflicts of interest that could have influenced its selection, editing, or publication.

References

Acosta A (2006) Breve Historia Económica del Ecuador.pdf. Corporación Editora Nacional. http://www.flacsoandes.edu.ec/libros/digital/42390.pdf. Accessed 24 August 2024

Assis Clímaco D (ed) (2020) Aníbal Quijano. Cuestiones y horizontes: de la dependencia histórico-estructural a la colonialidad/descolonialidad del poder. CLACSO, Bienos Aires

Becoña E (2006) Resiliencia: definición, características y utilidad del concepto. Rev Psicopatol Psicol Clín 11(3):125–145

Borja-Nuñez R (2011) Los movimientos sociales en los 80 y 90. La incidencia de las ONG,la Iglesia y la Izquierda. Centro de Investigaciones CIUDAD, Quito

Cabanyes Truffino J (2010) Resilience: an approach to the concept. Rev Psiquiatr Salud Ment 3(4):145–151. https://doi.org/10.1016/j.rpsm.2010.09.003

Carrión F (1986) De la manipulación de la esperanza a la gestión del fracaso:la triste historia del plan techo. Ecuador Debate 10:103–113. https://repositorio.flacsoandes.edu.ec/handle/10469/7899. Accessed 5 January 2023

[19] According to the Barranquilla sociologist Orlando Fals Borda, a "sentipensante" is a person who is capable of tuning the heart to reason. This relationship between feeling and thinking is presented by Fals Borda based on narratives taken from Colombian coastal culture (Fals Borda, 2002). In stories, tales, and histories, the "hicotea" turtle appears; during the dry season, it exhibits aestivation behavior, meaning it buries itself and survives on its reserves until the rains come. Aestivation is associated with the ability to resist shown by the men of this region. Sentimental men and women, who are capable of resisting and recovering from adversity, reflect in an exercise of harmony with nature. This is a tribute to the many "sentipensante" men and women who live in the region and who, in these times of adversity, just like the "Hombre-hicotea" or "hicotea-man," know how to endure and face life's setbacks by combining reason and love, body and heart, to rid themselves of all the (bad) formations that dismember this harmony and be able to speak the truth. A truth that emanates from popular knowledge and the relationship with nature and culture. It is also an invitation to look again at deep-rooted, cultivated, and proper thinking, which allows us to find the reason that was lost and disconnected from the heart, perhaps since the times of invasion and colonization. It is also a call to raise the voice, the same voice that was silenced, mutilated, excluded, and discriminated against; the voice that is now silent.

CEPAL (2023) Deuda pública y restricciones para el desarrollo en América Latina y el Caribe. Naciones Unidas, Santiago
de Santos BS (2009) Una epistemologia del sur: la reinvención del conocimiento y la emancipación social. CLACSO, Buenos Aires
de Santos BS (2010) Descolonizar el saber, reinventar el poder. In: Boaventura de Sousa Santos. Trilce, Montevideo
del Aguirre MR (1980) La acción habitacional del Estado en Guayaquil. 1972–1979. FLACSO, Quito
Dudley E (1986) La casa es lo primero: logros y falacias. Ecuador Debate 10:35–52
Fals Borda, O. (2002). Historia doble de la Costa 1: Mompox y Loba (2.ªed.). Universidad Nacional de Colombia, Banco de la República, El Áncora Editores. https://isbnsearch.org/isbn/9583600903
Kotliarenco MA, Cáceres I, Fontecilla M (1997) Estado de arte en resiliencia. Organización Panamericana de La Salud. https://www.paho.org/Spanish/HPP/HPF/ADOL/Resil6x9.pdf. Accessed 7 November 2023
Lopez Bracamonte F, Limón Aguirre F (2016) Componentes del proceso de resiliencia comunitaria: conocimientos culturales, capacidades sociales y estrategias organizativas. Rev Latinoamericana Cien Psicol 9(3):1–13. https://doi.org/10.5872/psiencia/9.3.61
Martínez-Molina V (2007) Arquitectura moderna en Quito 1950–1960. Universidad de Cuenca, Cuenca
Martín-Mayoral F (2009) Estado y mercado en la historia de Ecuador. Desde los años 50 hasta el gobierno de Rafael Correa. Nueva Soc 221:120–136
Moncayo V (2015) Orlando Fals Borda, Una sociología sentipensante para América Latina. Siglo Veintiuno, Buenos Aires
Oquendo L (1986) Expansión urbana y acceso a los sectores populares al suelo. Ecuador Debate 10:65–102
Palermo Z (2009) Conocimiento "Otro" y Conocimiento del Otro en América latina. Estud Rev Centeo Estud Avanzados 21:79–90
Paz, Miño Cepeda J (1994) La historiografia economica del Ecuador sobre el s. XIX y XX en los ultimos 25 años. Procesos Rev Ecuatoriana Historia 5:75–115
Ponce A, Valencia H (1981) Configuración del espacio regional ecuatoriano y desarrollo urbano de Quito y Guayaquil. Cuadernos Ciudad Soc 6:1–41
Quijano A (2014) ¿Bien vivir?: entre el 'desarrollo' y la Des/Colonialidad del poder. Cuestiones Horizones VI:847–862
Quintero J (2018) El conflicto social e historias de vida: la génesis del liderazgo y de la resiliencia comunitaria. Rev Reflexiones Saberes 9(1):58–73
Rodriguez L (1989) Las mujeres de Solanda: mujer, barrio popular y vida cotidiana. CEPAM-ILDIS, Quito
Suárez-Giordano L (1994) La Unidad de Valor Constante (UVC). Ecuador Debate 31:165–168
Tapia G (2012) Resiliencia: entre la crisis y el valor. In: Disertaciones XXXII Jornadas Nacionales de Administración Financiera SADAF, pp 259–308
Uriarte Arciniega JD (2013) La perspectiva comunitaria de la resiliencia. Psicol Polít 47:7–18
Van Sluys C, Jaramillo E (2021) La memoria de la materia. Una historia contada en concreto. Dinediciones, Quito
Zhingre R (2020) Quito: una organización territorial en las que se expresan características especulativas excluyentes en la década de 1980. Sociología y Política Hoy 2:26–40. https://revistadigital.uce.edu.ec/index.php/hoy/article/view/2524. Accessed 3 September 2024

This Never Ends: The Everlasting Conflict Between Debt, Spatial Growth, and Home Beautification in Solanda and Carapungo

Andrea Pacheco Barzallo, Marco Lenin Lara Calderón, and Mauricio Unda Padilla

Abstract This work aims to study the interrelationships between indebtment and different spatial expressions or needs in popular territories characterized by a combination of self-construction and planning techniques. With this purpose a qualitative methodology was implemented through 25 in-depth semi-structured interviews with groups of inhabitants of two neighborhoods which were chosen for being highly representative and emblematic examples of the architectural and urban condition of the social habitat in Quito; also, within its territories, walking tours were conducted to identify the landscape and spatial expressions reported by the interviewees. In this document, we report the results obtained regarding the spatial categories or typologies considered as the motivators for the acquisition of debt identified in the case studies.

Keywords Indebtedness · Spatial consolidation · Female debt · Migration

1 The Tale of Two Neighborhoods

One of the effects of Ecuador's first "oil boom" during the 1970s was the design and implementation of massive housing projects, mainly in Quito and Guayaquil. Population growth and internal migration generated the so-called "urban housing deficit," allowing certain "social" or "minimum" housing concepts to emerge in the country (Acosta 2009a); these concepts are still in force today. The investment programs resulted from state and private initiatives, often with funds from international loans. Due to this process, important parts of Quito underwent intensive construction based on this housing type and its transformation over time.

A. P. Barzallo (✉) · M. L. L. Calderón · M. U. Padilla
Faculty of Arts, Design and Architecture, International University of Ecuador (UIDE), Quito, Ecuador
e-mail: anpachecoba@uide.edu.ec; mlara@uide.edu.ec; maundapa@uide.edu.ec

A. di Campli (ed.), *Inhabiting Debt*, The Latin American Studies Book Series,
https://doi.org/10.1007/978-3-031-99886-7_3

From the 1970s onward, several financial booms were accompanied by the development of large-scale housing and infrastructure projects. The country's political, economic, and social environment shaped a regional regime of power (in so-called developing countries) encompassing all spheres of life, including housing, food, health, education, and the media. This led to the establishment of patterns and norms regarding the definition of "poverty" or "family," which tended to place the "middle and lower classes" in circuits of consumption.[1]

1.1 Solanda

This was the context when the Solanda Housing Plan was implemented in the southern part of Quito; it covered 150 hectares at 2800 m asl, near the *Quito Sur* ravine. The land was part of the *Hacienda Marquesa de Solanda*. In 1976, María Augusta Urrutia donated the land to the Mariana de Jesús Foundation (Kueva 2017). In alliance with the *Junta Nacional de la Vivienda* (National Housing Board), the foundation was jointly created in 1973 by the military government of Guillermo Rodríguez Lara, the Agency for International Development (AID)—an international cooperation agency of the United States government—and the Municipality of Quito; the foundation designed, financed, and implemented a model neighborhood project, based on "progressive" housing concepts (Ferguson and Navarrete 2003). The beneficiaries of the project took out thirty-year mortgages and became indebted to the *Banco Ecuatoriano de la Vivienda* created in 1961.

Officials of the Mariana de Jesús Foundation made several visits to Chile and Colombia, which were reference countries regarding "social" housing based on a "developmental and modernizing" vision. The Ecuadorian architects Adolfo Olmedo, Ernesto Guevara, and Walter Moreno were in charge of the final project in Solanda. It was presented as a collective housing project during a competition at the first Biennial of Architecture of Quito in 1978 where it did not receive any recognition.[2]

[1] The construction of model neighborhoods, such as Solanda and later Turubamba and Carapungo, was also a strategy by the State and the Municipality to counteract the widespread land invasions and the wave of informal housing construction that took place in the south and north-west of Quito. In turn, these sectors constituted germinal spaces for popular political organizations.

[2] The economic crisis in Ecuador in 1998–1999 was an inflationary crisis combined with a financial crisis, a fiscal crisis, and a sovereign debt crisis that began in 1998 and continued to worsen, leading to a banking panic in 1999. During the inflation in 1998 (52.6% average annual devaluation), the Central Bank of Ecuador issued excessive national currency (Ecuadorian sucre), depreciating its daily value. This was done not only to cover both the fiscal deficit of the State and the current expenses of the public sector, which were aggravated by the 75% drop in the price of oil (a product that in 1998 represented roughly 22% of the state's income), but also to inject bailout funds for the banks, some of which passed into the hands of the Ecuadorian State through the AGD (Deposit Guarantee Agency).

Solanda was built as part of a broader geopolitical agenda for "development" and "poverty" control; it was promoted, within the framework of the "Cold War," as a way to "curb" the emergence of insurgent movements in the region. Some features of the project triggered speculation regarding land values in surrounding private areas, the establishment of minimum housing standards, the choice of construction systems based on incremental or progressive processes, the layout of communitarian spaces, and long-term indebtedness intended as a social discipline tool operating in economically poor environments.

The district of Solanda has 24,526 houses, a density of 176.2 inhabitants per hectare, and 4.8 inhabitants per lot. The plots measure 60 m^2 and 120 m^2 (Merizalde Zapata and Lara Calderón 2022). The urban structure comprises four neighborhoods divided by two perpendicular axes, forming a four-quadrant grid in which two neighborhoods are located to the north and two to the south of the district. The settlements to the north are made up of eight super-blocks, each divided by a green fringe with services, whereas the neighborhoods to the south consist of 16 super-blocks, each divided by José Alemán Street, also known as "La J." Each neighborhood also has small-scale service buildings that dynamize its interior. The super-blocks in *Solanda* are built based on the linear typology. These types are the sum of built lots classified into three types: corner, townhouse, and "bridge." Moreover, these typologies embody multifamily housing units that can have up to two floors, progressive single-family houses, mixed-use houses with shops that can have two floors, and the "bridge" typology with integrated places for crafts.

The government primarily delivered a 24.11 m^2 housing type known as *Vivienda Piso-Techo* (floor-ceiling house) to its inhabitants. These houses had a lower concrete floor, columns, a roof, and a sanitary unit; they sometimes included internal walls. According to Lilia Rodríguez (1990), a sociologist and political scientist specializing in gender issues, 4212 out of the 5600 houses in Solanda (75%) were delivered in precarious conditions. Four other types were designed for the Solanda Housing Plan, offering different options depending on the credit capacity of potential beneficiaries. A more basic unit than the *Piso-Techo* was the *Vivienda tipo L.U.S, Lote Urbanizado con Servici*o, a 10.46 sqm lot with a sanitary unit and skeleton. The *Vivienda Trifamiliar,* built on minimum lots of 92.16 or 122.88 sqm, was offered to the more affluent. One of the most interesting types of *viviendas*—that still influences the neighborhood's transformations over the years—is the *Vivienda Puente* type, built on 24.09 m^2 and designed as a mixed type: housing combined with commercial space for productive uses. Finally, a type called *LUV-2B, Lote urbanizado con Vivienda* (Urbanized Lot with Housing) was also offered, with one or two floors; it was the only complete unit in the complex and was intended to serve as a model for all the others (Rivas and Ramón 2018; Salazar et al. 1989).

During that period the economic situation in Ecuador was marked by migratory waves of Ecuadorians to Spain, Italy, and the United States; this was a consequence of the political and economic crisis that led to the so-called *feriado bancario* crisis

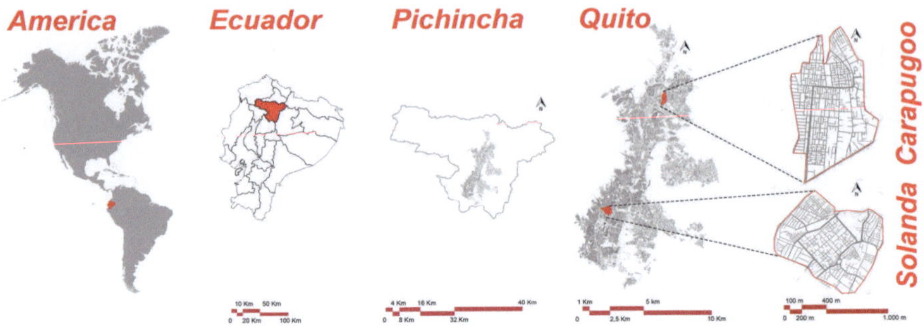

Fig. 1 Case study location

in 1999.[3] This crisis triggered the emigration of millions of Ecuadorians, many of them *solandeños* (*Solanda's inhabitants*); thanks to the work of these peasants who migrated and sent remittances which led to several different kinds of transformation in Solanda. For example, the proliferation of small businesses such as grocery and prepared food shops, especially in Calle J (José María Alemán), gradually became the iconic feature of these enterprises (Fig. 1). Another change occurred in the grouping and visibility of young people from migrant and non-migrant families; thanks to their music, occupation of public space, and graffiti, they established a new territoriality throughout the South, marked by new borders and the advent of micro-powers linked to social, aesthetic, and generational disputes. Other vital resources that allowed Solanda to grow and become consolidated in the 1980s and 1990s were the *mingas*,[4] neighborhood organizations, neighborhood councils, improvement committees, and associations—many led by women—that were created to demand the State to provide basic services such as drinking water, lighting, public spaces, road paving, and transportation (Ramón Navarrete 2017).

The occupation of Solanda's structures has changed from 100% single-family residential use with a service fringe area to mixed-use on the first floors and multi-family housing. The mixed-use houses are primarily located at the intersections of passageways and vehicular streets. However, the most significant change in Solanda was its architectural overflow. The self-building, extension, and recycling undertaken by most residents transformed the 1978 urban design, revealing new landscapes and, thus, new poetics. The original Solanda plan was intended for 20,000 people, but estimates now reflect that approximately 130,000 people currently reside in Solanda due to the influx of migrants from rural territories, as well as Colombia, Cuba, and Venezuela. Additionally, this district has a floating population of between 35,000 and 40,000 inhabitants. This makes Solanda one of the areas

[3] In addition, the systematic injection of large-scale corporate capital in the south for the construction of shopping centers, multiplex cinemas, supermarkets, and transnational food and clothing chains created intense pressure on the community. The community's economic and social fabric is intense but fragile, based on the 'day-to-day,' reflecting the inequalities and dynamics of the market.

[4] See di Campli in this book.

with the highest cultural density, turning it into the epicenter of life in the southern area of Quito (Kueva 2017; Morillo-Aguilar and Lara Calderón 2023; Rivas and Ramón 2018). In just two decades, Solanda became fluid and dynamic, characterized by an assortment of uses and social groups that bestowed multiple meanings on the neighborhood.

Similarly, the Carapungo neighborhood, located in the northern part of the city, is characterized by a highly changeable, evolving urban landscape. It is difficult to identify the patterns or objectives of its initial planning scheme since alterations and self-construction have surpassed any functional, aesthetic, or constructive intentions of the planners.

1.2 Carapungo

Carapungo is a neighborhood located to the north of Quito and is part of the parish of Calderón. Its urbanization began in the 1980s after the implementation of one of the social housing programs launched by the central government. Specifically, the urbanization process (17 hectares of arid land with a dry climate and no agricultural vocation) was part of the program with which the Christian Social regime and the former mayor of Quito, and later president, Sixto Durán Ballén, intended to fulfil part of the slogan "Pan, Techo y Empleo" (Bread, Housing, and Employment) of his presidential campaign. Acosta (2009b, p. 50) states that it was during the 1970s and 1980s that the "flagship programs" of Rodrigo Borja's government were implemented, namely Carapungo in Quito and Los Sauces in Guayaquil. These programs were aimed at the middle and lower-middle classes (Acosta 2009a; Jaramillo González 2009). As far as the Carapungo urbanization process is concerned, the state acted as a real estate agent and intervened in the real estate market.

He maintains that as a real estate agent, the State—owner of the land—established its use and defined social housing, granting credits through the *Banco Ecuatoriano de Vivienda*[5]; as an intervener in the real estate market, the State exploited the housing program to spark other collateral processes, such as the production of an urban space dominated by the formal real estate market (sale and renting of housing). The dwellings in the right sector of the neighborhood were provided by the social housing program. The blocks in this area have a similar structure; the impression is of a labyrinth due to the similarity of all the houses and the narrow 6-m-wide streets. These houses had been designed for low-income social sectors. However, the initial design did not satisfy the needs of those to whom the houses were allocated, thus resulting in transformations. The most common housing type is the terraced house. In the left sector, after receiving "assurances," the State granted land on which each owner built according to his needs and tastes. The fact

[5]The Ecuadorian national institution was created to provide the poorest Ecuadorian population with facilities to obtain long-term credit to either purchase or build their own homes.

that the Carapungo social housing program did not satisfy several architectural and urban needs prompted groups of neighbors to organize and create the Comité Pro Mejoras de Carapungo in the late 1980s. Transformations became visible; several houses began to be enlarged; the growth was vertical and involved the construction of several floors while the façades were painted in different colors; other alterations and additions were also implemented. The transformations of the urban surroundings involved basic services, mobility, and infrastructural needs.

During the 1980s, the Carapungo neighborhood was inhabited by people from different parts of the country; after that decade, it became a destination for migrants. The *fuereños* (outsiders) arrived in the neighborhood when it was already "consolidated" with all the services and facilities; however, they were not property owners. The presence of national and foreign migrants made the whole commercial area economically more dynamic; it is central in terms of its relationship with adjacent neighborhoods in the parish of Calderón. Carapungo is currently a place characterized, in particular, by Afro-Ecuadorian urban territorialization due to the historical process of appropriation and domination during which the Afro-Ecuadorian population in the neighborhood tried to build it as a "good" space to live in. As a result, Carapungo is part of a network of specific territories in Quito's metropolitan area linked to an urban network of Afro-Ecuadorian neighborhoods.

1.3 Objective and Methods

After reading the analysis of the reasons identified in the literature explaining the processes of housing transformation in the built environment, it is easy to understand how they are related to the gradual emergence of a series of unmet needs that trigger modification processes. These phenomena—widespread in Ecuador and in the rest of Latin America and our region—have increased drastically in recent decades (Mosso 2019). In many countries like Ecuador, the spatial modification of social housing is an essential process illustrating the ability of low-income housing to adapt and grow sustainably according to the changing needs of its residents. This issue is important; it is a survival mechanism in areas where urban populations continue to grow, and the lack of affordable housing is a constant challenge. This individual expression of self-improvement is because "social or popular housing" designs or logic are not intended to respond to each family's unique and changing needs in a broad and constantly evolving process of inhabitation over some time. Planning alone is unable to anticipate these needs; together with regulatory and control deficiencies in the construction of the habitat, this results in the unlimited transformation of neighborhoods (Durán et al. 2020; Rodríguez and Sugranyes 2004), especially when the logic behind Latin American social housing has historically been considered as a space for self-construction due to economic and family reasons and the need to respond urgently, thus requiring gradual adjustments to these pressing unmet needs (Gelabert Abreu and González Couret 2013; González 2006).

For low-income populations, for whom saving is not a feasible option, the processes of change and the ability to satisfy needs within the home also entail a parallel process of indebtedness with banks, cooperatives, relatives, friends, employers, or other informal entities. This indebtedness often exceeds repayment capacity; as a result, people urgently need to find creative ways to meet their acquired obligations. Moreover, obtaining and coping with debt becomes a housing production model that deserves to be understood in-depth so that innovative policies and mechanisms can be developed, allowing families in need to meet said needs over some time. Therefore, our study aims to identify the main spatial modification processes that lead to the indebtment of families in popular neighborhoods of Quito. Aiming to carry out a deep analysis, a qualitative approach was implemented through a case study methodology. The research team selected the Solanda and Carapungo neighborhoods as representative or emblematic examples of the architectural and urban conditions of the social habitat in Quito. Two cases were selected to gather data from the two extreme geographic areas of the city, the north, and the south; each of these geographical poles is strongly characterized at the cultural, social, and economic levels, generating two different imaginaries of the city (Fig. 2).

Two activities were carried out in both cases: in-depth semi-structured interviews and walking tours. Between the two cases, 25 interviews took place with groups of inhabitants who bought their houses by incurring debt; these exercises lasted around an hour each and included visiting the houses, observing the dwellings, and identifying the changes that, over the decades, have transformed the landscape of the neighborhoods; also, during the interviews, documents, and photographs to support the testimonies, were collected. All participants were informed about the project's objectives before each interview and signed an informed consent form. The walking tours were conducted in the public space of each neighborhood to identify the landscape and spatial expressions reported by the interviewees.

Interviews from both cases were transcribed, coded, and analyzed using the qualitative research software ATLAS.ti. A first reading of all transcripts was made for the coding process, and eight codes were defined among the research participants based on the main ideas identified: demographics; origin, evolution, and debt

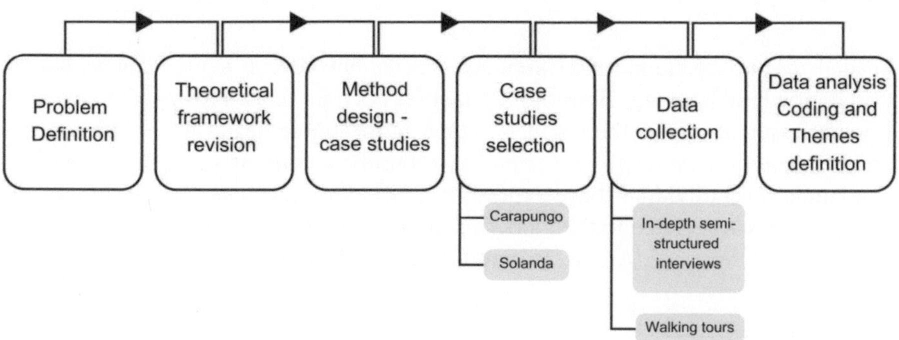

Fig. 2 Research Methodological structure (by the authors)

policies; planning and spatial needs; debt actors; formal and informal aspects of debt; social community struggle; cultural aspects of space and debt; perceptions and feelings. During this process, similarities and differences in results were also analyzed; however, it is worth mentioning that both cases were observed under the same process and code structure.

A thematic analysis followed the codification process, targeting different readers and publications depending on the results obtained. In this document, we report the results obtained regarding the spatial categories or typologies considered as the primary motivators for debt acquisition in the case studies: three-dimensional consolidation of space, debt for the construction of productive spaces and economic security, debt for the aesthetics of the home, and debt due to multigenerational cohabitation.

2 Indebtedness and Space in Solanda and Carapungo

Most of the inhabitants in Solanda and Carapungo have been forced to implement housing extensions over a period. As stated by Durán et al. (2020), these extensions were built by taking advantage of setbacks and inventing many structural and construction solutions, often designed to tackle problems such as the shortage of living space. One of the most common strategies has been to build new rooms or enlarge existing housing by adding more floors upstairs. In some cases, this required a radical reconfiguration of the housing structure or the construction of annexes, something that often entailed significant costs.

The following considerations focus on these processes; they are organized in two parts. Part one presents the most relevant spatial characteristics of debt in the Solanda and Carapungo settlements. Part two discusses the differences in the relationship between debt and space between the two contexts.[6]

2.1 *Debt for a Three-Dimensional Consolidation of Space*

An analysis of the Solanda and Carapungo settlements reveals a crucial aspect of the spatial growth of housing. Household growth is not only related to unsatisfied needs; in many cases, it can be the result of either an insatiable desire for expansion and improvement or the nurturing of personal or family wealth; on more than one occasion, numerous individuals have expressed a will to improve their living status. This eagerness may be related to the modernist architectural guidelines of the 1960s that were adopted by Latin American countries; in fact governments built collective

[6]The research team selected the Solanda and Carapungo neighborhoods because the processes of indebtedness were spatially evident in these areas.

housing projects based on "progressive housing" parameters (Merizalde Zapata and Lara Calderón 2023); the underlying idea was that, when economic resources were available, it was possible to increase the functional space. Theoretically, this growth follows predefined patterns inherent in the project plan. However, the landscapes of many neighborhoods, such as the ones examined in this study, show that this planning pattern eventually disappears. The desire for growth is also revealed as being something that goes beyond the functionality of the dwellings; it has to do with new aspirations, new generations, new aesthetics, and spatial interpretations. Moreover, when housing is considered as a process, growth and adaptations occur when its inhabitants are ready, without greater control, without being predefined, and without an estimated timeframe for completion; instead, housing is considered as the result of a long process linked to indebtedness, the extinguishment of old debts, and the acquisition of new debts.

> …This process is never really finished. I will die, but I won't finish building the house. Yes, a lot is missing. One thing is always missing, and another thing, yes, for example, I'm telling you... the... outside I need to level the floor of the... the floor of... the laundry room, I also need to plaster the walls of the laundry room and upstairs on the terrace I need to do the same with the furniture of the things I have. So, there is always something missing, but I'm doing everything, little by little, little by little. Everything you see here is done by me except the television.
>
> (A neighborhood resident, personal communication, 2022)

When talking to participants and observing the current landscape of the neighborhoods, the spatial pattern that appears can provide clues about how the spaces were consolidated. There is a clear tendency to expand and consolidate homes in a three-dimensional manner, designing layouts linked to the optimization of the internal space and aiming for maximum functionality. Maintaining empty spaces is not a rational option when it's possible to enlarge one's dwelling. When resources are found, rooms are enlarged, and "unusable" spaces are enclosed. New terraces are created; although often incomplete or partially covered, these terraces correspond to new usable surfaces. Open space and green areas remain only outside, in public areas, or on roofs that can later be used to create new rooms or apartments. The façades reflect this tension toward a three-dimensional increase in housing. The front façades of the row houses develop, as far as possible, into public space. The style of the buildings is cubist—clear, defined, massive volumes, the construction of which marks the final phases of the building processes based on debt mechanisms (Fig. 3).

In both case studies, volumetric growth and the consolidation of homes define the neighborhood landscape; however, slight differences do exist between the two cases. In Solanda, greater growth and an even more prosperous neighborhood life has persisted to the present day. This is because the exponential growth of the population (from 20,000 to 130,000 inhabitants) has led to intense construction in Solanda, ignoring the formal harmony between "full and empty" spaces; moreover, this has led to a lack of complementary elements for neighborhood life, such as recreational and green areas. On the contrary, in recent decades, the proliferated construction of closed residential complexes in Carapungo has generated a radical

Fig. 3 Exteriors of the homes in the Carapungo area (by the authors)

change in the possibility of transforming homes because these new territories are more formal and follow the features predefined by designers and co-owners of said complexes (Pacheco Barzallo 2022).

2.2 *Debt for the Construction of Productive Spaces and Economic Security*

> See, since I lived on rent, I suffered being a tenant; it's not the same thing. So, feeling the house as my own is different until we start to build and live, as they say, decently; then, we begin to develop an affection for the space and try to start. I have a story; for example, my husband had a friend whose parents were elderly and didn't have a house. It was such a sad situation, and it hurt me so much that when they were already elderly, they must have been at least 60–80 years old, they were saying: 'Hey, even just a small room and a kitchen, you have to help us find something for rent.' Imagine, this struck me deeply, and I said no, for my old age, I seek my own home.
>
> (A neighborhood resident, personal communication, 2022)

Debt has become deeply rooted in Ecuadorian culture as a fundamental tool to meet housing goals, improve lifestyles, and perhaps acquire material goods. The interviews reflected the fact that debt is, therefore, the primary tool to achieve individual and family emancipation; it enables people to build their future and also that of future generations. Debt is, therefore, a process that will continue throughout life, increasing in proportion to one's desires and goals. However, those who live in debt are chained to a life of memories from the past, daily challenges, or situations that disrupt the normal development of an individual, family, or home. Comfort is not an option but a projection and expectation pursuant to the sacrifices that prioritize the family's needs in a house—a home that simultaneously provides the opportunity to either create new spaces for productive activities, generate income, or rent out spaces. Many of these spaces, located on the ground floor, result in neighborhood amenities such as pharmacies, hardware stores, grocery stores, bazaars, liquor stores, workshops, etc. In both cases, homes have been seen to transition from 1 or 2 floors to 5, 6, or 7 floors with bedrooms or rental apartments. This spatial and commercial growth and increase in the population has also led to some public spaces, initially intended as places of recreation and interaction for the inhabitants, to be turned into parking lots.

Let's now focus on the historical processes that shaped Solanda and Carapungo. Recognition should be afforded to the consolidation of the current strength of these neighborhoods as economic engines, with beautiful commercial centers and road axes for many retailers. It is worth noting that this is the result of a process primarily driven by the efforts of the families that live there; this drive is more intense in Solanda than in Carapungo where commercial zeal has managed to replace functional housing in some areas. Planning overlooked several aspects of habitability and the generation of resources; this is simply the result of the residents' desire to have some kind of future economic security; said security was achieved through indebtedness and sacrifice. Thomas Carlyle stated: "*There are only two ways to pay debts: by working and by saving*" (Froude 1885) we can state that the inhabitants involved in the study cases did indeed agree with this statement since it is the most common method used by the people and families, who accessed a loan and acquired a housing solution in Solanda and Carapungo, to reach their goal (Fig. 4).

Fig. 4 Current state in Solanda (by the authors)

> At first, I only made it for living, so this part was the living room. I had the kitchen and the living room. That was it, but it turned out that my husband had his business in the centre, and since it was far away, he was gone all day. There was a meal problem; he couldn't come or go in time. So, we damaged the living room and divided it, and here is the workshop. Then, with the kitchen, I had to move upstairs to the terrace.
> (A neighborhood resident, personal communication, 2022)

So, indebtedness represents a necessary step, not only to be able to have a house, but also to be able to have and keep a job. It represents the opportunity to give oneself one's "own space" and transform and adapt one's needs in the present and future.

> People with limited resources generally get into debt to be able to have something, as they say; if you don't get into debt, you never get to have anything...
> (A neighborhood resident, personal communication, 2022)

2.3 *Debt for the Aesthetics of the Home*

Social housing, with its doctrines of functional and space optimization, has neglected qualitative aspects, giving way to a vast array of creative expressions through the tool of self-construction. The residents in Solanda and Carapungo who assumed an initial economic burden and debt in order to purchase their homes incurred additional debts to achieve their aesthetic intents or aspirations. Participants in the research repeatedly mentioned that they obtained resources to carry out "finishes," "facades," and modify "windows."

> …so, we received the house in '86. We were... because they handed it over to us just built, it had no repairs, not the facades, nothing...
> (A neighborhood resident, personal communication, 2022)

> …Of course, we had to take out loans to start fixing floors and walls, which were the main things.
> (A neighborhood resident, personal communication, 2022)

> As they say, you can't make it if you don't get into debt. But yes, I would do it again. But to improve the quality of life inside the house.
> (A neighborhood resident, personal communication, 2022)

> What has been done is painting, fixing; for example, those woods were, my God, it seemed like they had brought them from who knows where. They have been lacquered and maintained to give it that sort of tone. So, that's what has been done on the ceiling. Upstairs, it was just a warehouse…
> (A neighborhood resident, personal communication, 2022)

One may think that this rational and functionalist perspective is stronger than the logic of aesthetics; however, what the participants mentioned allowed us to establish that functionality and aesthetics are closely connected. What we must emphasize here is the fact that aesthetics follows cultural, social, and economic patterns. Several studies have made significant efforts to define the aesthetics of different groups; among them, "*feísmo*" has been considered as an aesthetics belonging to certain socio-economic classes where countless design ideas from various cultures and eras are mixed, where materiality and color play a fundamental role, and disorder is the design order in which recycling is critical to its materialization, providing important lessons regarding recycling and sustainability (López 2017; Palomares López 2018). This "*feísmo*" is perhaps a conceptual category providing a theoretical understanding of the aesthetic spectrum of the homes in Solanda and Carapungo. Since no specific order guided this design, creativity gave way to a diverse landscape with an extensive range of colors and different materials; this is visible chiefly on the front façades of the homes, while the side or rear façades may remain either without aesthetic finishes or be left with the raw material, potentially resembling temporarily attached precarious constructions whose image is very similar to that of informal settlements (Ducci 1997).

2.4 Debt Due to Multigenerational Cohabitation

Louis Kahn used to say: "The house is the abstract definition of spaces good to live in... a house is a conditional interpretation of spaces... different for each of its inhabitants" (Heil 2003). For the residents of Solanda, incomplete homes without finishes also became an embryonic family space, accommodating multiple family units (Fig. 5). This is why, on more than one occasion, they needed to incur debt and gradually build the spaces that could ensure a habitat for several generations.

> ...because, as I already had the three children, then thinking about them, I said the family will keep growing, and that's what happened... well, this and now there are grandchildren... of course, not all of them live here, but suddenly they all come, so the house fills up, even lacks space.
>
> (A neighborhood resident, personal communication, 2022)
>
> Let's say for my husband, building the house did cause conflicts because there wasn't enough, or we moved in without putting in the windows. We started with the bottom floor, then my in-laws passed away, and their inheritance was divided among the siblings, but that didn't serve as a foundation to build the second floor (Vargas, personal communication, 2022).

Numerous benefits are associated with spatial expansions in social housing; the chief benefit is the possibility of accommodating family growth, such as the birth of more children or grandchildren (Fig. 6). This triggers cohabitation between multiple generations in a single housing unit; the many advantages created by this situation

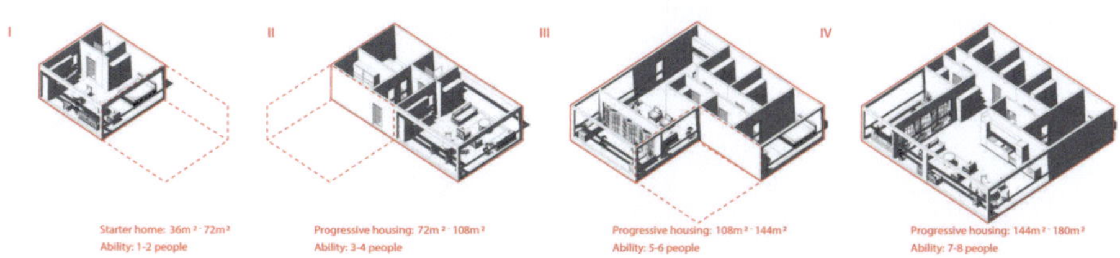

Fig. 5 Solanda. Progressive growth of the original planned housing (by the authors)

Fig. 6 The interior of multigenerational homes in Solanda (by the authors)

include assistance to ensure the economic sustainability of the household and support for the upbringing and care of children or elders, etc. Even when a family member lives elsewhere, homes allocate neighborhood safety spaces for all members in case they may need it at any time.

> Well, you see, I have mini-apartments. For example, downstairs, there is the storefront and two bedrooms. What the bank gave us, and I expanded it. I have four floors, but here, all my married children live... Well, my daughter-in-law and my son are out in Spain. So, here live, for example, my daughter-in-law with her little daughter, my son who was here with his girlfriend, my other son lives alone, but also has his small apartment, and then there's us, my husband who is downstairs, and me. So, around 7 people more or less.
>
> (A neighborhood resident, personal communication, 2022)
>
> …You see, I thought, no, one floor for each child, as I had three children, so I thought three floors and one floor for us.
>
> (A neighborhood resident, personal communication, 2022)

What emerges from the interviews is that indebtedness is not a linear process. It is an incremental and mixed process, and furthermore, it is not strictly connected to the value of the property (house). So, it is not only an economic investment but rather a relational one: it is the beginning of a relationship with a territory, it is the promise of building one's own identity in a specific neighborhood. The process of continuous transformation of the space, inside and outside the houses, of taking care of public spaces, of designing collective activities, and establishing a deep affective bond with the neighborhood. The accumulation of different forms of debt (formal and informal) creates a deep bond in the inhabitants and between the inhabitants and the neighborhood; it is one of the main and most original elements of the link between space transformation and indebtedness.

3 Solanda: Female Debt Work

Women, especially poor women, have become essential cogs in the wheel of indebtedness processes in Quito and in processes of the financial colonization of the habitat. Women are responsible for managing household debt, which has exploded over the last decade, reaching an all-time high after the recent economic and political crisis. Women in Solanda are overrepresented as clients and managers in numerous categories of loans (including subprime lending, microcredit policies, consumer loans, and rent and utilities) and are being enfolded into the system. Working-class women are at the forefront of the new forms of labor generated by this increased use of financing. As managers of family budgets, they find themselves monopolized by the management and refinancing of debts, not only the ones they have contracted but often the ones contracted by their families.

Managing debt in Solanda involves real work: routine and time-consuming tasks require special skills, and the configuration of areas used as domestic ateliers or commercial spaces. In places like Solanda, this "debt work" involves dealing with monthly, weekly, and even daily repayment transactions. It involves juggling five, ten, and fifteen loans at a time and keeping track of these skeins of debt through incessant mental gymnastics, which require complex calculations based on criteria of price and sentiment. Debt work often goes hand in hand with work for debt, aimed at finding the funds needed to pay the debts and interest, which are often exorbitant. In Solanda, this means longer working days, stretching into evenings and Sundays. People juggle two or three activities to keep the cash flowing in.

For women in Solanda this may mean working either outside the home, as a cleaner, or in the home, making clothes or preparing food sold at the market (Corrales Gallardo et al. 2022). This is the case for grandmothers who continue to work after retirement and use their access to credit to help their unemployed children.

Debt work and work for debt represent a huge source of dispossession for the working classes and profit for the financial services industry that relies on the free labor of women and the seizure of a considerable share of the family's income. These mobilizations show that "debt work" supports women's resistance and a political voice rooted in the everyday lives of working-class people.

While women are shadowy players in the finance world, they are also fervent opponents. In Ecuador, as well as in other Latin American countries, they are speaking out against the violence of debt and the excessive burden it puts on their shoulders. These women are actively campaigning not only for the debt to be cancelled but also for social policies that will eliminate this chronic indebtedness.

4 Carapungo. Migration and Debt

Debt and indebtedness are core issues in the lives of migrants in Carapungo. Indebtedness can trigger migration; at the same time, migrants can regularly use loans to finance costly cross-border moves. The remittances sent home by migrants are often used to repay household debt. The mixed economies of debt incurred by migrants are made simultaneously in different contexts and at different periods in time. In Carapungo, in particular, it is possible to pinpoint migrants' diverse debt ecologies; the latter cross multiple spatial and financial boundaries and include formal and informal practices. Debt plays a significant role in place-making activities undertaken by migrants and their families in the place they migrate to. A key factor behind sending remittances back "home" is to preserve the migrants' place in these communities by investing in land and housing; the latter is funded through a mixture of wages, savings, and borrowing, thus enabling migrants to pursue an almost universal ambition to return home in the future (Datta 2017; Zapata 2013). In turn, credit and debt also facilitate placemaking in host countries.

Furthermore, these ecologies of debt reflect how migration and debt are spatially and temporally co-constituted, encompassing people, communities, and institutions distributed across multiple sites and times. Debt shapes the nature of migration, determining dwelling practices and economies. Periods of mobility are interspersed with waiting times when new debt relations are forged to set in motion iterative migrations. In turn, as migrants travel, the nature of debt transforms itself in such a way that debts previously characterized by mutuality are experienced as monetary obligations. Our examination of migrants' engagement with debt highlights the micro-spaces of the home in which debt relations are created and managed. Together with debts incurred in the past, these engagements are shaped by the temporal ebb and flow of formal and informal credit.

Understanding migration as a financial practice sheds light on the space-times preceding mobility. In our research, while some participants insisted that their decisions to migrate were spontaneous—in response, for example, to a letter from a friend—for others, it loomed on the horizon as an inevitable reality arising from being caught up in protracted conflict. Notwithstanding, restrictive immigration regimes, increased costs, and the commercialization of migration mean that the resources required to mobilize this economy of desires invariably take time (Gammeltoft-Hansen and Sørensen 2013; Lindquist et al. 2012; Stoll 2010).

Migrants from financially excluded communities were much more reliant upon social relations to raise funds. In these instances, parents, siblings, extended family, and clan members emerged as creditors, raising funds by pawning jewelry and mortgaging, selling, or exchanging property. However, even unbanked migrants could sometimes draw upon formal financial resources through their diasporic networks. In turn, debt relations were stretched from the proximate to the distant, so much so that while some migrants drew upon locally situated social and financial capital, others benefited from credit lines extended by relatives across transnational space.

The migration of debt and migrants' debt ecologies, made up of diverse spatial and temporal practices, relations, and institutions, add a crucial dimension to the spatial politics of debt and credit. In this sense, separating informal from formal is problematic, given how these are entwined and sit alongside each other. This vision of the migration-debt nexus has the potential to structure more productive and generative politics of migration and debt.[7]

5 Conclusions

In cities like Quito, the struggle to acquire a home goes beyond having land and a building; the home becomes a changing space, a space of daily confrontation that grows and is transformed. It allows families to house multiple generations, regardless of the debt and sacrifice involved in the genesis of that space for new inhabitants.

This research indicates that it doesn't matter who contributed more, who sacrificed more, who worked more, etc. The most relevant aspect is the common goal within a family to own a property and make it a legacy of their own.

The results highlight that debt is a key mechanism for individuals, collectives, and families who use it to achieve their goals and make spatial modifications to face new challenges. This calls for innovation in mechanisms that reduce the formal and informal burdens of indebtedness.

Debt practices are diverse, and so is the quality of debts.

The different debt experiences observed in Solanda and Carapungo allowed us to question the space-times of debt in, and through, the city of Quito. We argued that indebtedness must first be understood as a spatial practice situated within specific spaces and times. Secondly, exploring debt through a spatial lens problematizes its political and social boundaries. Quito debt ecologies cross countless boundaries, such that formal/informal, economic/social, and market/nonmarket debts are entwined and sit alongside each other.

Transnational migration and debt are defining characteristics of contemporary society. In an era associated with both "unprecedented" mobility and over-indebtedness, moral panic abounds around both. At the same time, the link between the exploitation of the social condition of women and the financial system is also an increasingly evident and unavoidable contemporary condition. In this sense, it is simultaneously clear that indebtedness is a process that exploits women's incessant

[7] Cwerner (2001) acknowledges that 'migration has crucial temporal dimensions, and the often-overlooked fact that times migrate with people, that is, the time perspectives and symbols of immigrants affect in many ways their predicament in the host society.' Yet, arguably, migration scholars have chiefly presented time linearly and instrumentally, about return migration, temporary work, and permanent settlement (Griffiths et al. 2013). This shortcoming has been addressed in recent work exploring the interplay between time and migration (Bastia and McGrath 2011). Building upon an established geographical literature on time and temporality (Jeffrey 2008), there has been a renewed interest in how refugees, in particular, experience time.

care work. The two case studies are excellent examples of how women's daily work of caring for space, relationships, and the family economy produces new spatial forms. So, when Aitken (2015a, b), identifies debt as a "ubiquitous condition," he argues that it is the "most visceral everyday signal of the logic of financialization," i.e., a norm for a growing number of households underpinning both mundane consumptions as well as investments in the life course.

Production of the indebted habitat is the subject of this essay. The fact it is little studied is nothing new: amnesia has always existed regarding the political role of financial capitalism. Polanyi pointed this out as being present in the 50 years leading up to the 1929 crisis; we repeat it for the current crisis. The mechanisms behind this crisis, and the ever-increasing debts associated with globalization, have yet to be analyzed. It is still assumed that financial infrastructure is the basis of development, but we still need to understand that it reproduces crises. It reproduces itself through debt channeled into financial products that financial capitalism must continue to produce indefinitely, reproducing debt in an endless spiral.

Production of the indebted habitat is now, more than ever before, the plot to be understood and unraveled. Based on this idea, we can re-interpret the economy of debt, characterizing the contemporary urban and rural-urban economies of countries like Ecuador. In today's world, debt takes the form of the gigantic debts of states, companies, families, and individuals produced by the circulation of very high-risk financial vehicles, which people have progressively been led to rely on, get used to, and "believe in." Everyone is dependent on debt, because even those who are not capitalists or entrepreneurs, i.e., the vast majority of the population, are forced— for lack of a better way—to suffer the risky instruments of financialization.

The current impoverishment of the middle and lower classes in Ecuador is the result of this dependence on debt (mortgage, loan, honor credit, usury) and the devaluation of labor that has become unparalleled. The basis of trust in contemporary social systems has meanwhile become fragile; the social contracts of the past have broken down. The only thing left is to become indebted.

The current impoverishment of the middle and lower classes in Ecuador is the result of this dependence on debt (mortgage, loan, honor credit, usury) and the devaluation of labor that has become unparalleled. The basis of trust in contemporary social systems has meanwhile become fragile; the social contracts of the past have broken down. The only thing left is to become indebted.

How do we represent the existence of debt and overdue accounts in a world obsessed with affluence and plenty?

What does debt look like? It is not just a number on a past-due notice. Debt looks like a human being. As we have seen, debt has a precise emotional and relational dimension. It makes its way into the intimate sphere of every individual. It looks like a mother taking out a title loan on her car, it looks like a child denied nourishment because her parents owe the school "lunch debt." Or a senior citizen having their tax returns garnished to settle a judgment. Based on the analyzed case studies, we have concluded that in Ecuador, dwelling space and its production maintain a close relationship with processes of indebtedness, at least for lower-income classes.

Indebtedness is driven by an evolving desire for homeownership; it responds to family changes, aesthetic demands, and economic feasibility, as well as a desire to break free from the burden of renting.

However, we see that debtors are fighting back in Solanda and Carapungo. We hope that this alliance of debtors will grow and that they will be not only dignified but also defiant. The current economic system is unjust. Why should people be forced into debt because they want to learn or need shelter or food to eat? Why should debtors dutifully make payments when profiteers deny all of us the public services and protections people need to weather a pandemic, a depression, or whatever the next disaster might be?

In the end, what is at stake is our ability to find strategies to pursue greater spatial, social, and knowledge justice.

Competing Interest The authors of this chapter declare that they have no financial, institutional, or personal conflicts of interest that could have influenced its selection, editing, or publication.

References

Acosta ME (2009a) La gestión de la vivienda social en el Ecuador: entre la espada y la pared. Ecuador Debate Cuestión Vivienda Hoy 76:93–106. http://hdl.handle.net/10469/4185

Acosta ME (2009b) Políticas de vivienda en Ecuador desde la década de los 70: análisis, balance y aprendizajes, Maestría en Políticas Públicas con mención en Desarrollo Local y Territorio: 89. FLACSO, Quito. https://repositorio.flacsoandes.edu.ec/handle/10469/892

Aitken R (2015a) Everyday debt relationalities. Cult Stud 29(5-6):845–868. https://doi.org/10.1080/09502386.2015.1017147

Aitken R (2015b) Fringe finance. Crossing and contesting the borders of global capital. Routledge, Abingdon. https://doi.org/10.4324/9781315795713

Bastia T, McGrath S (2011) Temporality, migration and unfree labour: migrant garment workers. Manchester Pap Polit Econ 6:3–38

Corrales Gallardo NN, Pacheco Barzallo AC, Lara Calderón ML (2022) Espacio público, medio físico y percepción de inseguridad en el barrio Solanda. EÍDOS 14(19):25–33. https://doi.org/10.29019/eidos.v14i19.1017

Cwerner SB (2001) The times of migration. J Ethn Migr Stud 27(1):7–36. https://doi.org/10.1080/13691830125283

Datta K (2017) Mainstreaming the 'alternative'? The financialization of transnational migrant remittances. In: Handbook on the geographies of money and finance. Edward Elgar Publishing, Cheltenham, pp 539–561

Ducci ME (1997) Chile: el lado obscuro de una política de vivienda exitosa. Rev EURE 23(69):99–115. https://doi.org/10.7764/1164

Durán G, Bayón M, Bonilla Mena A, Janoschka M (2020) Vivienda social en Ecuador: violencias y contestaciones en la producción progresista de periferias urbanas. Rev INVI 35(99):34–56. https://doi.org/10.4067/S0718-83582020000200034

Ferguson B, Navarrete J (2003) New approaches to progressive housing in Latin America: a key to habitat programs and policy. Habitat Int 27(2):309–323. https://doi.org/10.1016/S0197-3975(03)00013-4

Froude JA (1885) Thomas Carlyle: a history of his life in London, 1834–1881, vol 1. Longmans, Green & Co, London

Gammeltoft-Hansen T, Sørensen NN (2013) The migration industry and the commercialization of international migration, vol 69. Routledge, Abingdon

Gelabert Abreu D, González Couret D (2013) Vivienda progresiva y flexible. Aprendiendo del repertorio Arquitectura y Urbanismo 34(2):48–63

González RAC (2006) Vivienda social y flexibilidad en Bogotá: ¿ por qué los habitantes transforman el hábitat de los conjuntos residenciales? Bitácora Urbano-Territorial 10(1):124–135

Griffiths M, Rogers A, Anderson B (2013) Migration, time and temporalities: review and prospect. COMPAS Res Resour Pap 3:1–31

Heil AL (2003) Voice of America: a history. Columbia University Press, New York. http://www.jstor.org/stable/10.7312/heil12674

Jaramillo González S (2009) Hacia una teoría de la renta del suelo urbano. Ediciones Uniandes, Bogotá. https://doi.org/10.57784/1992/40867

Jeffrey C (2008) Wait Environ Plann D 26(6):954–958. https://doi.org/10.1068/d2606ed

Kueva F (2017) CIUDAD MODELO: memoria del Barrio Solanda. https://www.paralaje.xyz/wp-content/uploads/2017/11/CIUDAD_MODELO_FOLLETO_24-10-2017.pdf. Accessed 6 June 2023

Lindquist J, Xiang B, Yeoh BSA (2012) Opening the black box of migration: brokers, the organization of transnational mobility and the changing political economy in Asia. Pac Aff 85(1):7–19. https://doi.org/10.5509/20128517

López AP (2017) Feísmo, una brecha en el paisaje gallego. Temas Arquitectura 8(1):155–176. https://revistas.santototunja.edu.co/index.php/tarquitectura/article/view/1623

Merizalde Zapata NV, Lara Calderón ML (2022) Vivienda como base para la creación de comunidades. Diagnóstico de la participación ciudadana en proyectos de vivienda social en Quito. In: de Madrid UP (ed) Seminario Internacional de Investigación en Urbanismo:14. Universitat Politècnica de Catalunya, Catalunya. https://doi.org/10.5821/siiu.12008

Merizalde Zapata NV, Lara Calderón ML (2023) Proyectar la vivienda no solo desde la individualidad, sino desde la comunidad. Reflexiones Sobre Vivienda Quito ESTOA 12(24):136–148. https://doi.org/10.18537/est.v012.n024.a11

Morillo-Aguilar NJ, Lara Calderón ML (2023) SOLANDA: "De lo planificado a la realidad de lo construido". In Sánchez Bellido AG, Rojas Vidovic JC, Aparicio Ortubé AC, Pazini Figueiredo EJ, Pedro Castro Borges P (eds) Memorias del XVII Congreso Latinoamericano de Patología de la Construcción y XVIX Congreso de Control de Calidad en la Construcción: 14, CONPAT 2023. Santa Cruz de la Sierra. https://doi.org/10.21041/CONPAT2023/V1CC5289

Mosso E (2019) ¿Pobre o empobrecimiento? Medición de las Necesidades Básicas Insatisfechas y localización de la población en Santa Fe. AREA, Agenda de Reflexión En Arquitectura, Diseño y Urbanismo:1–20. Universidad de Buenos Aires. Facultad de Arquitectura, Diseño y Urbanismo, Buenos Aires. https://www.publicacionescientificas.fadu.uba.ar/index.php/area/article/view/669. Accessed 18 March 2024

Pacheco Barzallo A (2022) Espacialidad de la Supervivencia para una Gestión Inclusiva del Riesgo de Desastres en Barrios con Características de Autoproducción del DMQ - Ecuador. Ph.D Thesis. E.T.S. Arquitectura (UPM). https://doi.org/10.20868/UPM.thesis.70721

Palomares López A (2018) Feísmo: lecciones de arquitectura y reciclaje. https://riunet.upv.es/handle/10251/102024. Accessed 8 April 2023

Ramón Navarrete P B (2017) Solanda, el caleidoscopio de la experiencia urbano-barrial, FLACSO Facultad Latinoamericana de Ciencias Sociales - Ecuador. https://repositorio.flacsoandes.edu.ec/handle/10469/13627. Accessed 10 June 2024

Rivas N, Ramón P (2018) El metro está pasando y Solanda se está hundiendo. https://www.academia.edu/37823088/el_metro_esta_pasando_y_solanda_se_esta_hundiendo_la_barra_espaciadora_pdf. Accessed 7 June 2024

Rodríguez L (1990) Las mujeres de Solanda: Mujer, barrio popular y vida cotidiana. Instituto Latinoamericano de Investi-Gaciones Sociales (CEPAM/ILDIS), Quito

Rodríguez A, Sugranyes A (2004) El problema de vivienda de los "con techo." Rev EURE 30(91): 53–65. DOI: https://doi.org/10.4067/S0250-71612004009100004

Salazar PM, Romero Paz I, Rodríguez Ramos J (1989) Cambios en las estrategias de vida de los habitantes del programa Solanda a partir de la adjudicación de la vivienda. In: Especialización para la investigación: pobreza, subempleo y estrategia de subsistencia en áreas urbanas. FLACSO - Sede Ecuador, Quito. https://repositorio.flacsoandes.edu.ec/xmlui/handle/10469/387?locale-attribute=en. Accessed 2 May 2023

Stoll D (2010) From wage migration to debt migration? Lat Am Perspect 37(1):123–142. https://doi.org/10.1177/0094582X09355430

Zapata GP (2013) The migration–development nexus: rendering migrants as transnational financial subjects through housing. Geoforum 47:93–102. https://doi.org/10.1016/j.geoforum.2013.03.010

The Impact of Debt on the Transformation of Social Housing Programs in the City of Loja, Ecuador

Andrea Ordoñez León, Claudia Costa-De los Reyes, Verónica Muñoz-Sotomayor, and María Fernanda León Vivanco

Abstract Financialization has become the main mechanism for accessing social housing (*vivienda de interés social, VIS*) in Ecuador, forcing low-income families to incur long-term debt to acquire basic housing which fails to meet their needs. This study analyses the relationship between debt and spatial transformations in two *VIS* programs in Loja: Ciudad Victoria and Los Geranios. Through spatial analysis and interviews, three main types of modifications made by homeowners were identified: (a) adaptations to improve habitability, (b) incorporation of productive spaces, and (c) formal changes for personal differentiation. These transformations respond to the need to correct deficiencies in the original designs, adapt to changing family dynamics, and generate additional income. The results reveal that between 50% and 90% of the buildings have been modified, affecting both housing habitability and the morphology of the neighborhood. The modifications require new financing, predominantly through savings or microcredits to escape from the financial mechanisms of bank loans. The study highlights the limitations of housing policies, recognizing the need to design a sustainable financing policy that recognizes flexibility as a key principle in the design of the *VIS*.

Keywords Social housing · Mortgage debt · Spatial transformations · Financialization

---

A. Ordoñez León (✉) · C. C.-D. los Reyes · V. Muñoz-Sotomayor · M. F. L. Vivanco
Faculty of Arts, Design and Architecture, Universidad Internacional del Ecuador (UIDE), Loja, Ecuador
e-mail: anordonezle@uide.edu.ec; clcostade@uide.edu.ec; vemunozso@uide.edu.ec; maleonvi@uide.edu.ec

A. di Campli (ed.), *Inhabiting Debt*, The Latin American Studies Book Series,
https://doi.org/10.1007/978-3-031-99886-7_4

1 The Issue of Housing Access: The Origins of the Indebtedness of the Poor in Ecuador

Ecuador is a country of 17 million inhabitants (INEC 2022) with a quantitative housing deficit of half a million housing units (Murillo 2021); as a result, access to housing is a crucial challenge faced by both the state and low-income families. To address this long-standing problem, social housing programs (so-called *VIS*, or *vivienda de interés social*) have been enacted, financed and/or subsidized by state authorities and implemented through housing policies in order to provide the population with "decent housing" (Ministerio de Hábitat y Vivienda 2021). According to Fernando Carrión (1996), the housing problem in Ecuador can be considered a structural phenomenon related to four causes: (1) accelerated urbanization processes in place since the second half of the twentieth century; (2) a social structure characterized by marked socio-economic inequities; (3) limited social investments due to accumulated public debt; and (4) shortage of land resulting in urban dynamics marked by speculation. These statements were made almost 30 years ago, however, even today, these causalities are still valid (Acosta 2009, 2022).

The development of *VIS* housing programs in Ecuador focused on legal regulations, state policies, and financial dynamics for access to housing, but not on issues such as functionality, comfort, or the satisfaction of housing users. According to Alcívar Macías et al. (2018), although the structural causes of the housing deficit were well known, policies were designed and implemented according to a reductionist analysis based on the quantitative deficit and not on qualitative aspects. At the same time, the design of the *VIS* housing programs did not diversify architectural typologies and spatial layouts or consider criteria of flexibility, adaptability or progressivity (Bamba-Vicente 2020).

According to state housing policies, access to housing was possible after a qualification process validating housing applicants to access mortgage loans intended to be feasible for the target population (Rodas Beltrán 2013). In this sense, access to the *VIS* involved long-term financial commitments, representing a serious economic effort for individuals and families; nevertheless, it has been noted that modifications or extensions were made to the houses after purchase, thus implying new debts or investments.

The urban standards of the *VIS* programs, their locations, times, costs, and even how housing was delivered, has been an important area of research for many Ecuadorian urban researchers (Durán et al. 2020). However, no studies have been performed, at least in Ecuador, either on the relationship between housing alterations and debt, or regarding the consequences of debt in the daily life of *VIS* populations. Considering that social housing is intended for those with low-income, and that a bank loan is required to access it, we can easily realize how alterations to housing—whether internal, external, aesthetic, or structural—can compromise not only the family's economy, but also the habitability of inflexible housing.

Held (2000) states that the main objectives of social housing policies in Latin America should initially be aimed at providing fair access to housing for low-income households, and that this housing must meet adequate standards in terms of lot size, basic amenities, floor space, materials, and finishes. Secondly, social housing policies should pursue housing cost containment objectives by testing efficient construction processes, providing public support policies for acquisition through subsidies, and calculating the beneficiaries' investment capacity over a period of time. State-promoted housing is often characterized by inexpensive architectural and construction solutions which, however, hardly ever satisfy the needs of families that then convert them over time, increasing both their indebtedness and the quality of housing conditions (González Couret and Párraga 2019).

An analysis of *VIS* programs in Ecuador shows that in order to reduce costs, the programs have been implemented in areas far from urban centers, without essential community facilities or adequate access to public transport. These implementation practices negatively affect the quality of life in social housing neighborhoods (Rodas Beltrán 2013; Durán et al. 2020). The state's logic of considering only issues of quantitative deficit and global economic dynamics has resulted in the production of living spaces that are neither adapted to forms of community life in the neighborhood nor take into account the difficulties of low-income people to move around and access public facilities and services (Hermida et al. 2019). In addition, the state has not considered family dynamics, specifically Latin American dynamics, related to the extended family or the changing needs of women, young people, immigrants, children, single parents, etc. (Hermida et al. 2019).

A study conducted on the paradigmatic case of the PREVI neighborhood in Lima, Peru, suggests that social housing in economically unstable countries becomes a platform for physical transformations that allow its inhabitants to address multiple socio-economic problems. Furthermore, incremental interventions enhance the property, the neighborhood, and even the city (García-Huidobro et al. 2010; Pérez and González Couret 2011). The study of social housing contexts in Chile by Greene and González (2011) focuses on the production of social housing from an incremental perspective, highlighting the issue of "unplanned incremental housing," which includes both expansion and improvement of the original dwelling.

We can therefore affirm that social housing programs in Latin America represent a policy that responds quantitatively to a deficit; it is not a spatial project, but rather an economic product designed for a generic population, made up of amorphous silhouettes, without specific needs but easily conditioned and controlled through a process of necessary indebtedness.

The real neighborhood design process begins only when people become owners of these spaces; during the lives of the individuals and families who participated in this design process they continually modify and adapt living spaces according to their changing needs and possibilities (González Couret and Párraga 2019).

The study conducted on a paradigmatic case such as the famous PREVI neighborhood in Lima, Peru, suggests that social housing in economically unstable countries becomes a platform for physical transformations that allow its inhabitants to address multiple socio-economic problems; furthermore, incremental interventions to adapt housing units produces an enhancement of the property, the neighborhood and the city (García-Huidobro et al. 2010; Pérez and González Couret 2011). The study of social housing contexts in Chile by Greene and González (2011) focuses on the production of social housing from an incremental perspective, highlighting the question of ‘unplanned incremental housing’, including both expansion and improvement of the original dwelling.

Reflecting on these topics, Peñaloza et al. (2019) highlight that the perception of indebtedness varies according to factors such as income level, gender, and age. In the case of lower income groups and the female gender, debt tends to be linked to expenditure and consumption. Moreover, in families with traditional structures in which the woman assumes the role of housewife, it is the man who generally meets the requirements for accessing credit in financial institutions, even if with the “joint credit” option (i.e., together with his spouse). In such circumstances, single mothers and divorced or separated women may find it more difficult to cope with monthly payments; this is the case of one of the interviewees and is corroborated by data from Global Findex (Demirgüç-Kunt et al. 2022) stating that in Ecuador only 14.5% of credit applicants to the financial system are women, compared to 32% of men. In other cases, prepayment may seek to release the mortgage, allowing the home to be used as collateral to obtain new loans to invest in home improvements or for other purposes.

In Ecuador, borrowing from financial institutions is an uncommon practice. According to the World Bank’s Global Findex (Demirgüç-Kunt et al. 2022), 47% of Ecuadorians have borrowed money, 29% borrow from family and friends, and only 23% borrow from financial institutions. However, in the capitalist process of financialization, the only way to acquire housing is to become involved with banks and be subject to credit, as stated by Ross (2017). In terms of access to housing and housing conditions, debt is the stepping stone to home ownership, but also to a loop of new formal and informal debts. Despite the official presentation of the *VIS* programs as a “turnkey” solution, this is only the starting point regarding housing, one which evolves over time in a generally unplanned incremental manner (Greene and González 2011). Housing actions are incremental, not only solved by new debts, but also through microcredits, savings investments, or extra income. Financing the transformation with savings could be a good strategy to avoid the risk on the property and save on bank interests; however, investing savings in housing disrupts the economy of the families, so that they will have to resort to indebtedness for other items such as health, mobilization or education. The flight from debt or the rejection of debt reflects the financial violence (Cavallero and Gago 2020) that pressures *VIS* beneficiaries, primarily those who do not have a fixed income, to get into debt; going through debt is a form of resistance to a traumatic event (Thornton and Haiven 2019).

Although there are very few studies about transformation and its impact on habitability and indebtedness, studies by González Couret and Párraga (2019) and Bamba-Vicente (2020) show that the *VIS* housing contexts in Ecuador are modified both architecturally and vis-à-vis the neighborhood. This is corroborated by reports on the Right to Housing in Ecuador (Defensoria del Pueblo 2013); they state that housing programs developed for the working classes represent an asset that is used productively to help develop the family economy. For this reason, *VIS* housing programs in Ecuador can be said to have been identified as platforms for the transformation of architecture and the neighborhood, involving tangible and intangible issues related to the quality of life of individuals and families. However, the *Ministerio de Vivienda y Urbanismo* (Ministry of Housing and Urbanism) continues to implement housing policies and projects that do not provide the flexibility needed to assimilate the transformations that families will make when they dwell and inhabit their homes (González Couret and Párraga 2019).

Based on the hypothesis that all social housing neighborhoods undergo different transformations, this study focuses on identifying the relationship between debt and the transformations that both the house and the neighborhood undergo over a period of time. The research analyzed two *VIS* programs in the Ecuadorian city of Loja, namely Ciudad Victoria and Los Geranios. The research approach combined spatial analysis and observation, interviews with homeowners, and quantitative data analysis, at different scales. Our aim was to explore the financing of spatial transformations over a period of time and how they affect the habitability of housing, the morphology of the neighborhood and, finally, the everyday life of the inhabitants.

This chapter is divided into four parts. Part one illustrates a framework that addresses two topics: (a) the implications of mortgage debt as a mechanism of access to *VIS* housing programs, and (b) the urban and architectural features of social housing projects and housing units. Part two describes two case studies. Part three describes the results of the spatial process of alterations in relation to debt. Finally, part four presents a discussion and the conclusions of this study.

2 Social Housing and Indebtedness: A Reference Frame

The first social housing programs were implemented in Ecuador in the 1920s based on policies promoted by the municipalities, but it was not until the late 1960s that a real public housing policy was established (Bamba-Vicente 2020). The first stage of the social housing policy involved implementing a financial scheme based, on the one hand, on the collection of internal savings through a private cooperative and mutual system and, on the other, by the investment of public resources through the Banco Ecuatoriano de la Vivienda (BEV) and the Instituto Ecuatoriano de Seguridad Social (IESS), coordinated by the State through the Junta Nacional de Vivienda (National Housing Board) created in 1973 (Carrión 1996). In the 1970s and early 1980s, housing policies were very centralized, with the state playing a direct role and assuming all related functions; instead in the late 1980s and the 1990s there was a transition toward policies influenced by economic liberalism; this led to a reduction in state intervention (Acosta 2009).

When the MIDUVI, *Ministerio de Desarrollo Urbano y Vivienda* (Ministry of Urban Development and Housing), was created in the 1990s, preferential interest rates were introduced in collaboration with the private sector; the rates were based on the economic assessment of beneficiaries and their ability to pay according to their income and employment stability. This approach paradoxically excluded those who were more in need of help to access housing (Córdova 2015); for this reason the *Subsidio de Vivienda de Interés Social program* (Social Housing Subsidy) was subsequently established; its objective was to provide non-refundable bonds and credits to reduce the housing deficit in lower-income sectors (Rodas Beltrán 2013).

By the year 2000, when the economic crisis prompted Ecuador to adopt dollarization, the *VIS* programs practically disappeared. State and municipal social housing initiatives were resumed toward the end of the century. Financially speaking, the characteristics of these new social housing programs were preferential interest rates that benefitted private builders in particular, and policies of non-refundable bonds for beneficiary groups. In Ecuador, there is a latent deficit and, as already mentioned, the *VIS* presents problems since it does not satisfy the needs of families (Ospina and Erazo Espinosa 2009).

As concerns financing, the problem of access to housing sparked a debate on several issues, such as the forced participation of beneficiaries in the financial system and the influence of this participation on people's lives. Mortgage debt accompanies almost all social housing programs (there are segments with total housing subsidies), with both state and private banks; this leads to another of the issues under discussion—the indebtedness of a vulnerable and low-income sector for several years (Cavallero and Gago 2020).

This dynamic reflects a broader structural trend: *financialization*, as a process within the capitalist system, extends financial logic to all areas of life. It evaluates businesses, services, and individuals based on their capacity to generate value, while ignoring how debt traps households in long-term financial dependency (Medialdea García & Sanabria Martín, 2013). As a result, essential sectors like healthcare, social housing, and education are judged by profitability rather than social function (Thornton & Haiven, 2019).

The ideology of home ownership is deeply rooted in Ecuadorian society. It is a powerful mechanism of financialization, exclusion, and territorial dispossession in which, directly or indirectly, both central and local governments have played a key role in adopting various forms of the financed housing policy model, limiting or abandoning alternative forms of housing production, freeing up land for urbanization, and deregulating building and housing quality standards. As a result, public policies have abandoned the concept of housing as a social asset and the city as a public artefact, and have renounced the role of redistribution of wealth in order to become mechanisms for rent extraction, financial gain, and capital accumulation (Delgadillo 2018; Rolnik 2021).

The fact that the acquisition of a mortgage debt with private entities is one of the requirements for the allocation of social housing affects the management of the right to housing, since the beneficiaries of social housing must first be subject to credit. If housing is a basic right, it could then be said that debt is a sine qua non condition for access to this right. This is what Ross (2017) describes as 'creditocracy', where indebtedness becomes a prerequisite and fundamental requirement of life. He also argues that the private financial system is not interested in citizens paying off their debts, but rather in prolonging them in order to sustain the mortgage business. From this perspective, housing that does not fully satisfy needs is convenient for the system, since, despite paying off the initial debt, it is likely that the owners will need to apply for new loans.

In this context, Cavallero (2021) argues that debt is a form of financial violence based on the denial and exploitation of the interdependence between creditor and debtor. Although the promotion of 'lower' interest rates are part of social housing policies, beneficiaries will contract more consumer debt or microcredits, at higher interest rates, to not only cover personal expenses, but also to complete the construction of a house that is not delivered in its entirety. Under the assumption that the beneficiary belongs to a vulnerable social group, and is therefore eligible for the *VIS* benefit, it can be assumed that the debtor will live for 15–20 years with a reduced basic salary and a financial obligation compromising his or her economic growth. In addition, trying to reduce construction costs often compromises the quality of the building, resulting in functional and even structural problems, and thus new expenses for the already indebted beneficiaries.

Argentina is an excellent example of the effects of financialization; its massive indebtedness occurred in the last decade, precisely when "social benefits became mediated by banks and individuals, which displaced other modalities of resource allocation" (Cavallero and Gago 2020, p. 51). This shift reveals that financialization puts the most vulnerable sectors in a risky position by exposing them to the private financial system, which is often poorly regulated in its credit relations with these sectors. In the context of home purchases, many people take on debt without a full understanding of their rights and responsibilities, which often puts them at a disadvantage *vis-à-vis* sophisticated and diversified financial institutions (Buckley et al. 2016). Finally, debt becomes not only an issue of economic impact, it also directly influences people's emotional health. In his paper on debt, Harker (2021) mentions that the crucial defining character of debt is its ability to link the present with the past and the future, and that a constant state of debt can transform not only the materiality, but also the emotional experience of place. Debt dynamics are marked by the constant of debt repayment or debt collection. If debtors lose their source of income, at some point their household becomes a place of anxiety and conflict (Harker 2021); with this in mind, getting out of formal debt circles is an imperative for debtors (Thornton 2024).

3 Urban and Architectural Features of *VIS* Housing Programs

VIS projects in Latin America primarily adopt two urban typologies: blocks of flats surrounded by collective spaces and terraced houses on individual lots. In some cases, combinations of these typologies were proposed. However, when a mass production approach was adopted, crucial aspects related to creating a real urban space were often overlooked (Link et al. 2022).[1]

Since the key objective of *VIS* programs is to maximize the profitability of land, houses are designed with minimum standards as regards space and construction; when beneficiaries occupy these houses, the aforementioned conditions trigger a transformation phenomenon which, in turn, impacts the overall configuration of the housing complex (Aranda Dioses and Torres Caldas 2023). According to Ecuadorian regulations, governing social and public interest housing—targeting priority groups that are either poor or vulnerable as well as households located in the two lowest income quintiles (Ministerio de Desarrollo Urbano y Vivienda 2013; Reglamento de Vivienda de Interés Social e Interés Público 2022)—generates neighborhoods that encourage social as well as spatial segregation (Molinatti and Peláez 2017).

Despite the fact that national urban planning regulations include leisure and recreational areas, there is minimum provision of public spaces in *VIS* programs for parks and sports areas. It is important to remember that in *VIS* programs the street is not only a place of transit, but also a complementary and necessary space for the habitability of housing, establishing a close relationship between the house and the street (Torres-Pérez et al. 2016).

Studies like the one by Bamba-Vicente (2020) analyze how the inhabitants of social housing programs use and appropriate public space in response to the housing space deficit and the users' own economy; the study identifies various forms of occupation and mentions "spontaneous association units" (Bamba-Vicente 2020, p. 198). These units refer to the way the inhabitants of neighborhoods with public spaces develop activities that contribute to their precarious economy or unemployment; in fact, there are uses and appropriations that do not imply permanent occupation, but temporary occupation with self-managed social, cultural, commercial, or productive activities.

Housing as a universally recognized right represents the foundation of stability and protection for individuals and families and is also the center of social, emotional, and sometimes economic life. Therefore, in order to be satisfactory, it must have characteristics that ensure tenure, availability of services, affordability, habitability, accessibility, correct location, and cultural adequacy (Guzmán-Ramírez and Bravo-Patiño 2017; OACDH 2010). However, the prototypes of the housing solutions in the *VIS* programs have been designed based on standardization, spatial economy, and cost reduction, involving cheaper housing materials and urbanization (Guzmán-Ramírez and Bravo-Patiño 2017; Rodríguez and Sugranyes 2009).

The effort to address the quantitative deficit has led to the construction of *VIS* programs with low-quality housing not linked to social and cultural reality (Vera

[1]The social housing projects feature different typologies: single-family dwellings on a minimum plot with one or two floors, two-member family units (semi-detached or duplex), and multistory collective housing. In Latin America, sizes range from 25 m^2 to 72 m^2 (Baraya 2020). In Ecuador, a standard size of 49 m^2 has been established, comprising a layout that includes two bedrooms, a full bathroom, a living-dining area, a kitchen, and a laundry and drying space (Ministerio de Desarrollo Urbano y Vivienda 2018).

and Wainer 2018). For this reason, housing development models do not meet the needs of users; in some cases they were abandoned due to issues related to distance, structural problems, lack of basic services and equipment, insecurity, isolation, etc. This indicates that in these circumstances the financial and social cost of housing can be higher than renting better located houses (Arnold 2019).

4 Two Case Studies

For the purpose of the study, two *VIS* programs were selected in Loja, an intermediate city located in southern Ecuador (Fig. 1). Since 1970, Loja has experienced steady population growth due to internal migration processes; this has generated

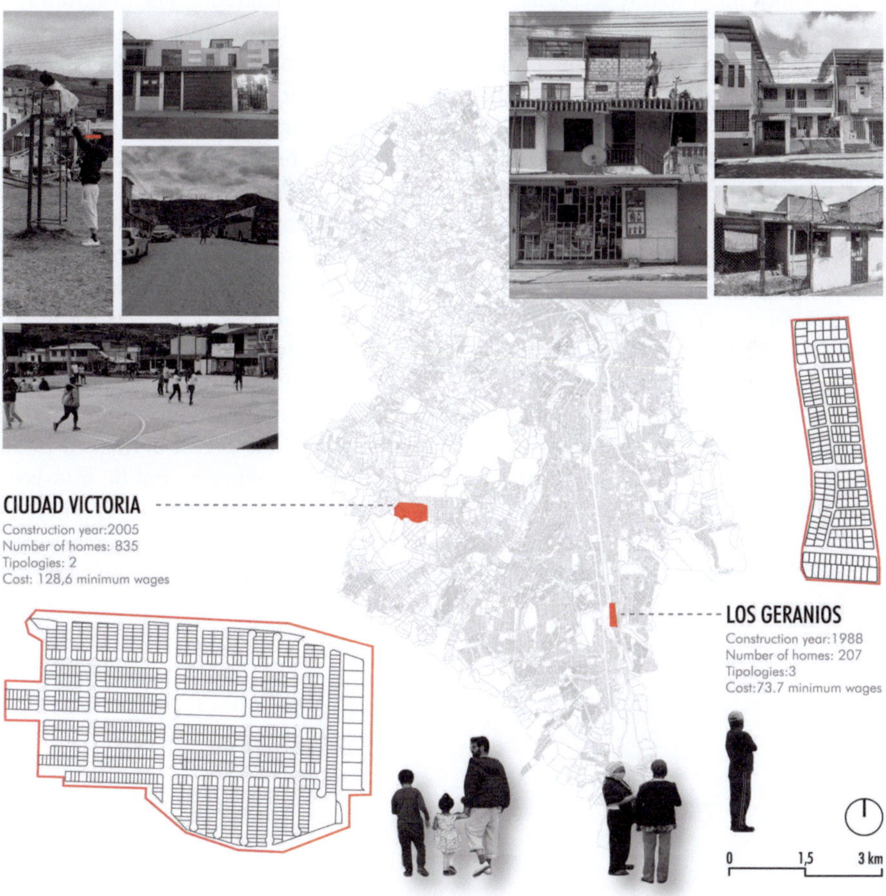

Fig. 1 Data and location of VIS projects (case studies)

increased demand for housing and urban expansion. In response, housing programs have been implemented, initially managed by the central government and, since 2005, by the local government.

The Los Geranios social housing program was developed between 1986 and 1987. The *Banco Ecuatoriano de la Vivienda* (BEV) promoted the program. The urbanization area is located in the southern part of the city, a sector that was being consolidated in the 1980s. The program included the construction of 500 dwellings based on the terraced house typology divided into one-family houses with one floor, one family houses with two floors, and two-family houses with two floors. These houses were delivered with an initial credit for 'shell and core work', without finishings and details; however, the beneficiaries could apply for other credits to finish the construction.

The 3.23 hectare urbanization polygon has a regular grid of rectangular blocks where single-family and two-family houses are distributed in rows; its road hierarchy includes main roads, secondary roads, and pedestrian streets. The program has a reduced communal area that is compensated for by the proximity of the linear park created after construction of the project. The architectural program did not envisage a garage; however the proposal included a communal outdoor parking area (Table 1).

The "Ciudad Victoria" housing program was the first municipal housing program; it was created in 2005 and promoted by the *Empresa Pública Municipal de Vivienda* (Municipal Public Housing Enterprise) (VIVEM EP) (Municipio de Loja, UTPL, GIZ 2018). The housing program was financed by the beneficiary, who participated with 30% of the value of the house, and a bond issued by the National Government; the rest of the debt was financed by local private financial institutions. Houses were delivered with basic services, in shell and core work. The program comprises 820 terrace type dwellings with one or two stories.

The neighborhood is located on a 15.6 hectare plot of land in the western part of Loja, 4.5 km from the city center. From the outset, accessibility to the neighborhood was limited due to its distance from the city center and the fact it is located in an semi-rural area. Ciudad Victoria is 40 min from the city center by public transport and 15 min by private car via the network of primary and secondary roads. There is a park in the center of the residential estate. The spatial layout correspond to a series of rectangular blocks created by sequences of terraced houses with front and rear setbacks.[2]

[2]Amazingly, the terraced typologies in grid-type blocks do not vary in the corner plots, where one of the façades retains the blind wall of the terraced construction. These characteristics highlight poor urban planning and design.

Table 1 Features of the housing programs under study

Attribute	Ciudad Victoria (polygon area: 15.6 ha)		Los Geranios (polygon area: 3.23 ha)		
Developer	Municipal Housing Company VIVEM EM		Ecuadorian Housing Bank (BEV) and National Housing Board (JNV)		
Planning year	2005		1986		
Plot area	90 m^2		85 m^2 and 70 m^2		
Setbacks	Front and rear		Front, rear, and lateral (corner plots)		
Housing typology and area	Single-story terraced house: 36 m^2	Two-story semi-detached house: 90 m^2	Single-story terraced house: 36 m^2	Two-story semi-detached house: 72 m^2	Two-family house (two floors): 36 m^2 per floor
Architectural layout	Living-dining room, kitchen, 1 full bathroom, 2 bedrooms, rear patio with laundry area	Living-room, dining room, kitchen, study, 1 full bathroom, rear patio with laundry area, 3 bedrooms, full bathroom	Living-dining room, kitchen, 1 bathroom, 2 bedrooms	Living-dining room, kitchen, 1 bathroom, 2 bedrooms	Living-dining room, kitchen, study, 1½ bathrooms, 2 bedrooms, 1 full bathroom
Cost	$13,000 equivalent to 74.3 SBU[a]	$22,500 equivalent to 128.6 SBU[a]		S/. 1,400,000 equivalent to 73.7 SBU[b]	
Financing	Owner 30%: $3900 BEV: $5000 grant private bank loan: $8900	Owner 30%: $6750 BEV: $5000 grant private bank loan: $10,750	Owner 10% BEV loan: 90%, optional BEV loan 1: finishes, optional BEV loan 2: extension		

[a] SBU of 2005
[b] SBU of 1988

4.1 Methodological Approach

The research addresses a sensitive and complex topic, as the acquisition of social housing is related to various aspects, such as families' purchasing and repayment capacity, housing as a vital space influencing the quality of life of its occupants, the opportunities it provides for participation in the productive and community sphere, as well as social interaction in public space (Fig. 2). Therefore, a mixed research approach was adopted. Semi-structured interviews, direct observation, and the collection of secondary information were employed. Through methodological triangulation, these tools and methods were combined to ensure the reliability of the study's conclusions (Carvajal et al. 2023).

Initially, a literature review was conducted, encompassing the exploration of scientific articles, regulations, and official reports related to the subject. Subsequently, a census was carried out through the collection of cadastral data applied to the 835 properties in Ciudad Victoria and the 207 in Los Geranios. The purpose of this

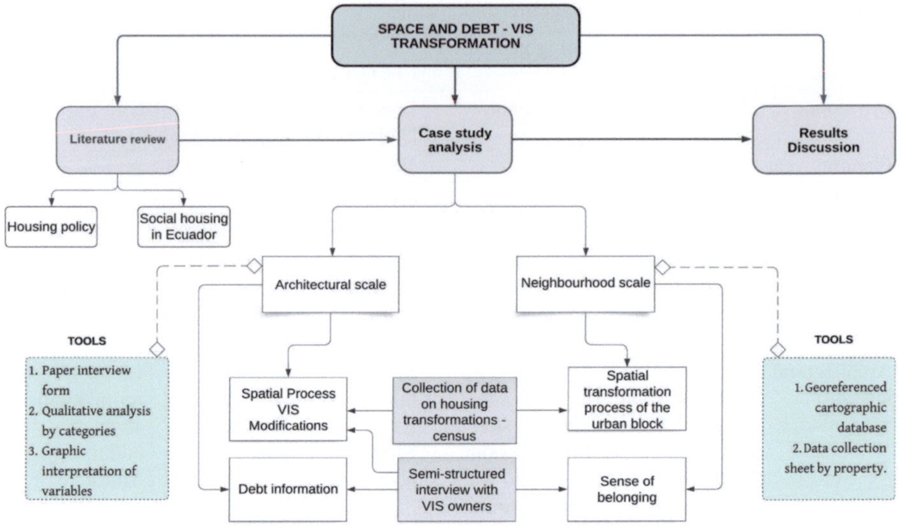

Fig. 2 Outline of the study methodology

census was to gather information on the occupation or vacancy of the dwellings, the modifications made to them, the occupation of setbacks with buildings, and the implementation of businesses or productive spaces within the housing units.

Following this, semi-structured interviews were conducted with key informants in each case study. Four owner-residents were interviewed for each case, focusing on four main aspects: (1) identifying data of the interviewee and family characteristics; (2) the financing of the initial housing and subsequent modifications; (3) transformations in the dwellings, the reasons behind these changes, their impact on family economy, and the use of spaces; and (4) perception of the neighborhood and community activities undertaken.

The urban characterization of the analyzed social housing programs was carried out using two approaches: a quantitative approach through morphological analysis of the transformation of the neighborhoods, and a qualitative approach through the conducted interviews. A categorization methodology was used to analyze the interviews. For the interpretation of the interviews, data coding was initially conducted, considering that each code is a word or short phrase symbolically representing a prominent attribute that captures the essence of linguistic or visual data obtained from interviews (Saldana 2013). In this way, for the study, the categories were associated with the analysis variables: indebtedness, spatial transformations, and the perception of family well-being. The refined interview data were systematically interrelated with the analysis categories, and in this manner, the interview results were interpreted.

5 Outputs: Housing Configuration and Collective Spaces—How the Local Population Re-designed the Space

This study collected both objective and subjective information. Apart from analyzing numerical data regarding housing and debt, we aimed to understand the complex interrelationships between the spatial configuration of VIS, access to housing through debt, and its impact on the daily lives of individuals and families (Fig. 3). The results are interconnected, revealing the significance of individual, family, and collective experiences linked to social housing.

In Ciudad Victoria, 47.3% of the dwellings have been modified. The transformation process is more noticeable in Los Geranios (Fig. 4, Table 2); in this case, all the dwellings have been altered, with 92.8% undergoing modifications and 48.8% occupying front setbacks, making it difficult to identify the original building type. The logic of unplanned incremental intervention (Greene and González 2011),

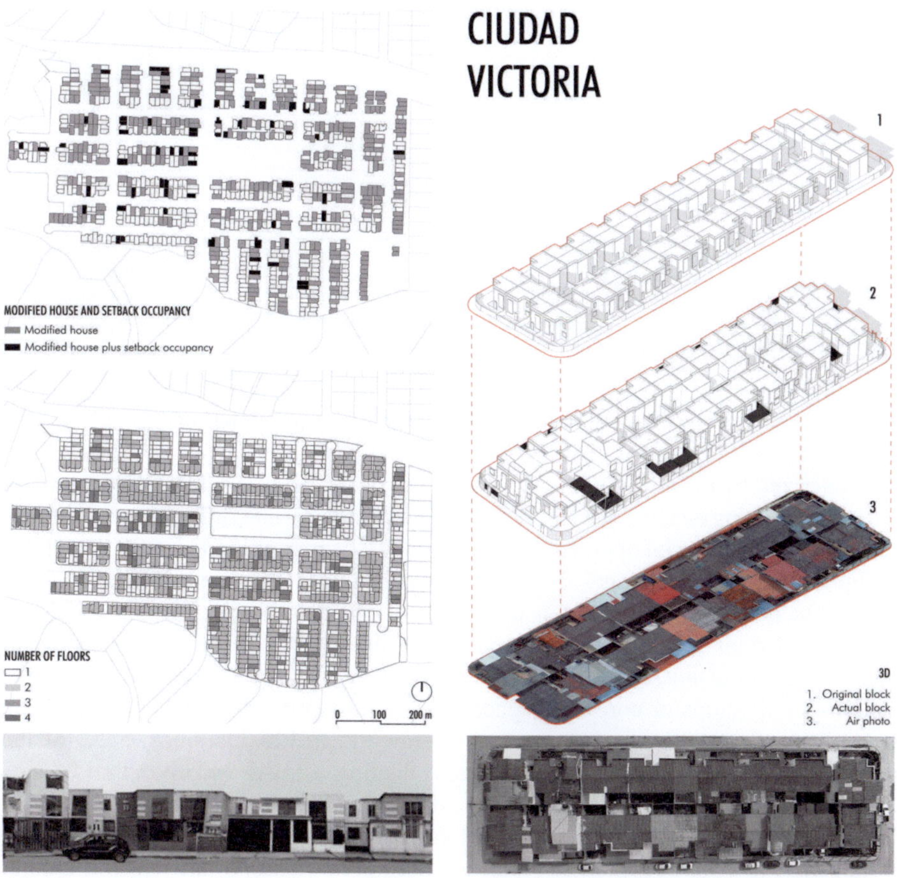

Fig. 3 Results of housing modifications carried out in the Ciudad Victoria program

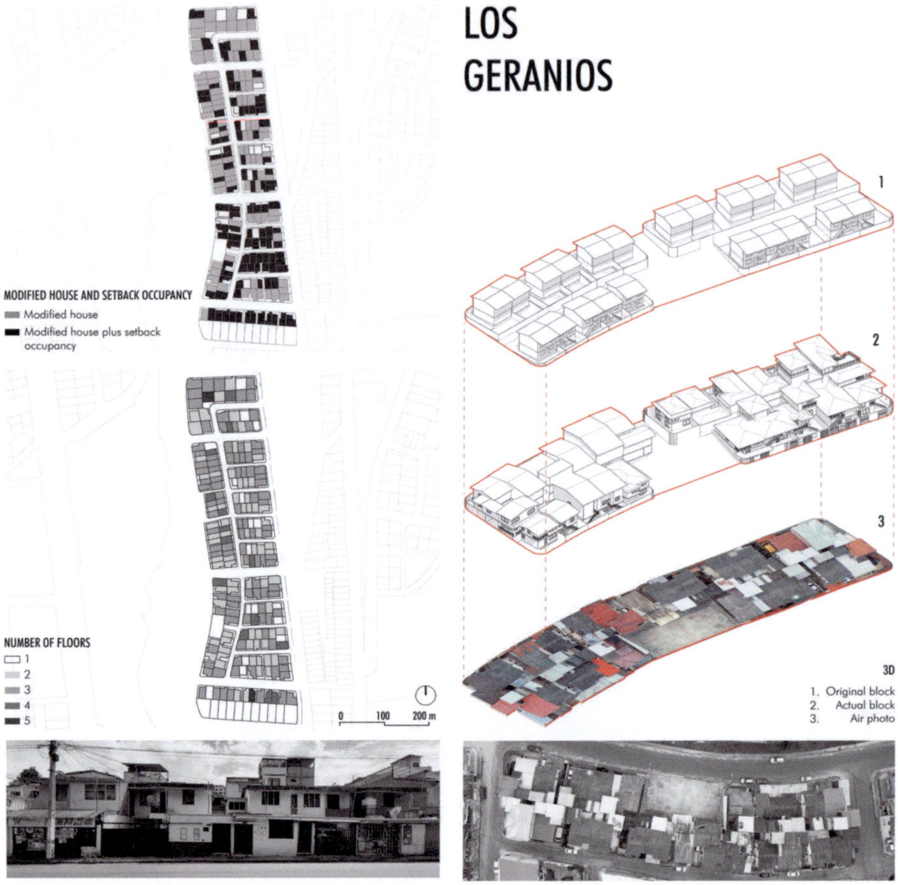

Fig. 4 Results of home modifications carried out in the Los Geranios program

characterized by the addition of new floors, the occupation of setbacks, or the renovation of existing spaces, has resulted in an urban image that differs from the original. The uniform, serial appearance has gradually been modified.

Furthermore, the changes inside the houses reveal "new productive spaces." These are primarily designed on the ground floor, combining domestic interiors with commercial activities, thereby redefining the relationship between the exterior and interior of the unit, as well as between intimate and collective spaces. Businesses such as small shops or corporate spaces are built to generate "new economies" in response to the incremental process of borrowing. In Los Geranios, 5.2% of the dwellings incorporate productive spaces, reflecting a lower incorporation of new uses than in Ciudad Victoria. This is because Los Geranios has been absorbed by urban growth and is surrounded by facilities, services, and activities complementary to housing. In contrast, Ciudad Victoria's peripheral location has led to a greater addition of productive spaces that provide services or fulfil needs unmet within the

Table 2 Case studies in numbers

Variable	Ciudad Victoria	Los Geranios
Urban space attributes		
Net population density	400 inhabitants/ha	340 inhabitants/ha
Total area	15.46 ha	3.23 ha
Public space (green areas, pavements, and roads)	50%	21.80%
Pedestrian public space (green areas and pavements)	32%	4%
Green areas	18%	0.15%
Number of housing units	835	207
Housing configuration (census)		
Occupied dwellings	90.40%	100%
Unoccupied dwellings	9.20%	0%
Modified dwellings	47.30%	92.80%
Unmodified dwellings	52.30%	7.20%
Dwellings undergoing modification	6.50%	0.00%
Dwellings occupying the front setback	7.30%	48.80%
Dwellings with a productive space	5.20%	7.70%

neighborhood or nearby areas. For example, 7.7% of dwellings incorporate local businesses such as shops, supermarkets, food stores, hairdressers, and hardware stores.

Regarding open spaces, in Ciudad Victoria, 32% of the total area is designated for pavements and roads, and 18% for green areas, which, however, are not considered public space. It is the residents who, by organizing themselves as a community, carry out "mingas,"[3] sell local food, organize bingo events, and make donations. Through their efforts, they have created sports areas and implemented improvements such as roofs, enclosures, and other enhancements. In Los Geranios, 21.65% of the total area is allocated to pavements and roadways, while only 0.15% is reserved for public space, which is practically non-existent within the neighborhood. In both cases, most of the existing sports and recreational spaces are maintained by the inhabitants as a means of improving the habitability of the urban area. They also manage various activities that strengthen neighborhood unity and increase their level of satisfaction, reinforcing their connection and sense of belonging.

This sense of belonging stood out in the interviews with the inhabitants of the VIS programs. One male interviewee stated: "In the neighborhood, the inhabitants have strong relationships with each other; for example, I play sports with my neighbors."

On the one hand, the inhabitants are aware of social problems such as insecurity, lack of facilities, remoteness from basic services or workplaces, and the inefficiency of the public transport system. However, these challenges do not generate disconnection, a lack of identity, or a negative perception of the neighborhood. On the contrary, the inhabitants develop deep ties with their place of residence (Fig. 5).

[3] See di Campli in this book, page 32.

Fig. 5 People's perception of the public space of VIS programs

In Ciudad Victoria, the recreational area is occupied by ecuavolley, football, and basketball courts—all sports played mainly by men.[4] Only 15% of the area is designated for a children's playground and an exercise area for adults. In this neighborhood, the management attempted to improve the space by installing exercise equipment and enclosing the children's area for greater safety. However, women and girls use this space less frequently than men and boys, as noted by one parent: "*Even in the children's area, only boys go. Also, I don't send my girls to the shop because of the dogs.*"

In Los Geranios, the importance of sports spaces is also evident in the improvised ecuavolley court created in the communal parking area. Additionally, the

[4] Ecuadorian volleyball or ecuavolley is a special type of South American version of volleyball.

inhabitants of this neighborhood have transformed pedestrian walkways into garages due to the lack of designated parking spaces in the housing models.

All these appropriations exemplify what Bamba-Vicente (2020) refers to as a "network of spontaneous territorial appropriations," which are linked to efforts to compensate for the deficiencies in the construction of social housing neighborhoods.

In the case of Ciudad Victoria, the distance between the neighborhood and the city center is a major issue. The inhabitants have found alternative solutions, as public transport takes up to 40 min to reach the city center. There is only one bus line, and its frequency is poor. For this reason, all the interviewees consider having a vehicle essential. Two interviewees bought a motorbike for their adult children to use when traveling to university. Another interviewee mentioned that they maintain a room in the city center, using it during the day and returning home only to sleep.

Regarding housing configuration, the study analyzed eight dwellings, revealing that VIS housing models were designed based on a family unit of four or five people with medium-low economic income and access to the national financial system. The housing was constructed with minimal space, no capacity for physical transformation or flexible use, and was delivered in substandard conditions due to a lack of finishes and built-in furniture necessary for adequate habitability. Six of the interviewees moved into the house as it was and made necessary repairs after their arrival, while two completed renovations before moving in.

Observations showed that the spatial configuration of the dwellings complicated cohabitation among different family members, as most families exceeded the average family size. The modifications made by users went beyond formal consolidation of the dwelling and involved spatial and technological adaptations based on family dynamics, economic resources, and the owners' debt capacity. In some cases, dissatisfaction with the dwelling led to its abandonment, negatively impacting the surrounding environment. In Ciudad Victoria, 9.2% of the dwellings were identified as abandoned or unoccupied.

The analysis of housing modifications examined the reasons for these transformations and how they were financed. Results revealed that formal alterations were made when the buildings were handed over to the owners, who carried out their "completion," including cladding, painting, flooring, and carpentry (Table 3).

From a functional and technological perspective, the study identified intervention patterns related to the occupation of building setbacks, which affected the lighting and ventilation of interior spaces. Horizontal extensions on the ground floor were primarily driven by the need to incorporate spaces for work or production, as well as to expand social or service areas.

Another common alteration was the addition of extra floors to accommodate new bedrooms and bathrooms due to an increase in family members. These alterations were undertaken without consideration of how they might compromise the structural stability of the buildings, particularly when carried out without technical supervision. All interviewees confirmed that they had made modifications without professional oversight (Fig. 6).

Table 3 Modifications to social housing

Formal modifications Formal consolidation	Finishing works in dwellings	Coatings, paint, flooring
	Incorporation of elements	Interior doors
	Addition of complementary services	Internet, cable television
Functional modifications Adaptations—extensions	Interior changes in the dwelling	Kitchen and dining room extension, additional bathroom
	Exterior extension of the dwelling	Incorporation of productive spaces, bedrooms, service areas, kitchen
Technological modifications Adaptations—extensions	Construction systems	Installation of new structure
	Installations	Adaptation of installations for new spaces

Access to *VIS* housing programs implies indebtedness, which can have lasting effects on families' living conditions (Datta and Jones 2001), especially when the housing fails to meet their needs and requires further modifications. In Latin America, as well as in Ecuador, housing undergoes constant transformation, requiring financial investment at various life stages. Initial indebtedness is necessary to acquire housing through the national financial system, but it remains unclear how subsequent modifications are financed. Sources of funding may include new mortgage loans, family savings, remittances, or other financial mechanisms.

5.1 The Reason why Debt Changes the Living Space

The study demonstrates that the rigid concept of state-produced housing does not adequately respond to users' needs, as these evolve throughout the dwelling's lifespan due to the diverse lifestyles of families and how they are structured.

Based on the responses provided by the interviewees, several factors influence the understanding of debt processes about the continuous modifications undergone by the buildings: the financial context, access to credit, and the owners' saving capacity. These aspects significantly impact housing transformations and the criteria for their configuration. On the one hand, inhabitants seek to consolidate the dwelling and meet the needs of the family nucleus; on the other, some modifications reflect an effort to showcase the family's economic standing. The findings illustrate how, through the routine of living, debt manifests and becomes an integral part of the "evolution" of both the dwelling and the inhabitants' way of life (Fig. 5).

An analysis of the link between spatial production processes and domestic debt in the two case studies reveals that the housing transformations are mainly based on three rationale.

The first incentive is "adaptation for habitability." These incremental alterations are often obligatory due to the conditions in which the acquired housing is

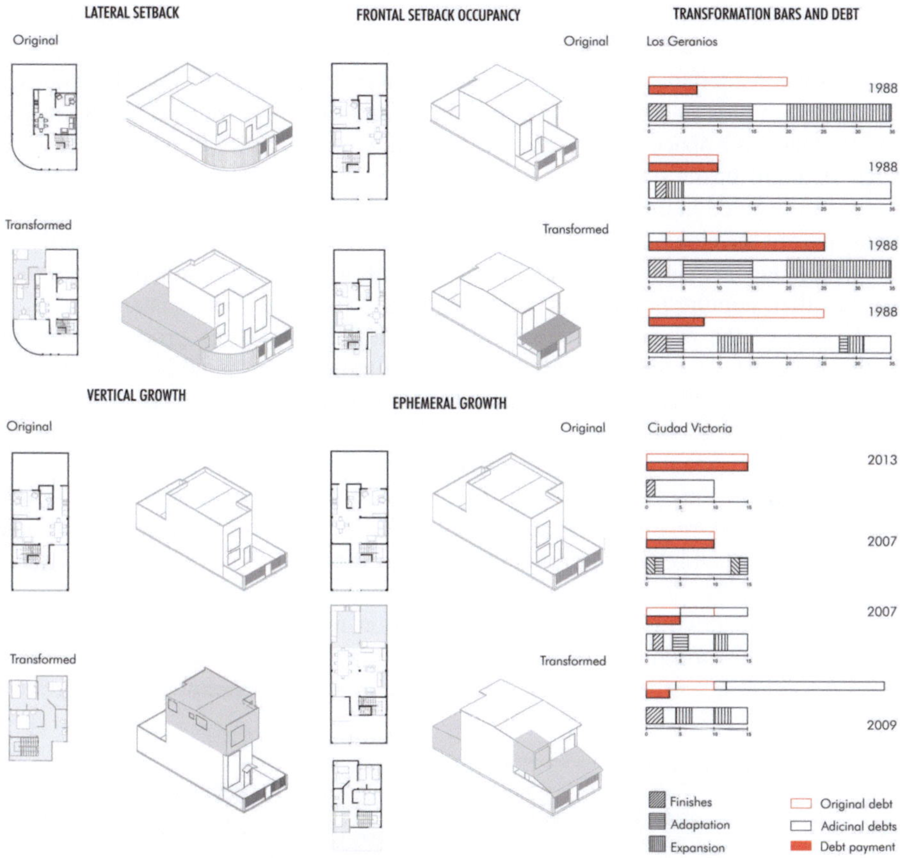

Fig. 6 (left) Summary of the different types of building transformations in VIS programs. (right) Temporal relationship between transformations and indebtedness

delivered. Most of the interviewees contracted their first additional debt within the first 5 years of acquisition. In the years that followed, the house was extended and modified according to each family's specific needs and circumstances. For example, the front and rear setbacks of the dwelling are sacrificed to either incorporate missing or nonexistent spaces such as bedrooms, bathrooms, and productive spaces, or to expand existing spaces that are insufficient for adequate habitability. During the 2020 pandemic, many families renovated their domestic spaces. One of the interviewees commented that " the kitchen space was initially very small, it was changed four times to enlarge it, and also enlarge the bedrooms." According to Florencia Partenio (2022), these actions can be considered as debts of care. With regard to the effects of financial vulnerability in working-class households, it is precisely the multiple spatial management of care that sustains the social reproduction of life; it does this by assembling spaces and infrastructures, by activating community and kinship networks and also by avoiding falling into new cycles of indebtedness.

The second incentive refers to adaptations related to the "development of popular microeconomics." When families create productive spaces or new housing units for rent, they consider spatial transformations as an investment rather than an expense. The Los Geranios and Ciudad Victoria neighborhoods are precisely as much a space of resistance as a space of exploitation, marked by the presence of microeconomies such as small businesses or informal workshops. Generally speaking, productive spaces are located in the social area of the house, specifically in the living room and in the part of the frontal setback next to this room. These forms of economic activity reflect, on the one hand, forms of capital valorization and exploitation practices and, on the other, popular pragmatics corresponding to forms of debt resistance.

As part of the productive spaces incorporated into housing, grocery shops in Latin America emerge as unplanned opportunities for "neighborhood unity" (Zumelzu-Scheel 2016). Owners respond to local demand for basic necessities, particularly when residential areas are isolated from the urban fabric, as was the case in both neighborhoods studied. While productive spaces are not always a direct consequence of debt, they do stem from the dynamics of microeconomies, which are capitalized within residential spaces. Consequently, debt also influences the urban image and restructures the morphology of the neighborhood in response to collective needs (Fig. 7).

The last incentive is related to transformation for "spatial differentiations and improvements" carried out for pleasure and to satisfy personal taste. These alterations are often not urgent and involve specific items, for example, to change the

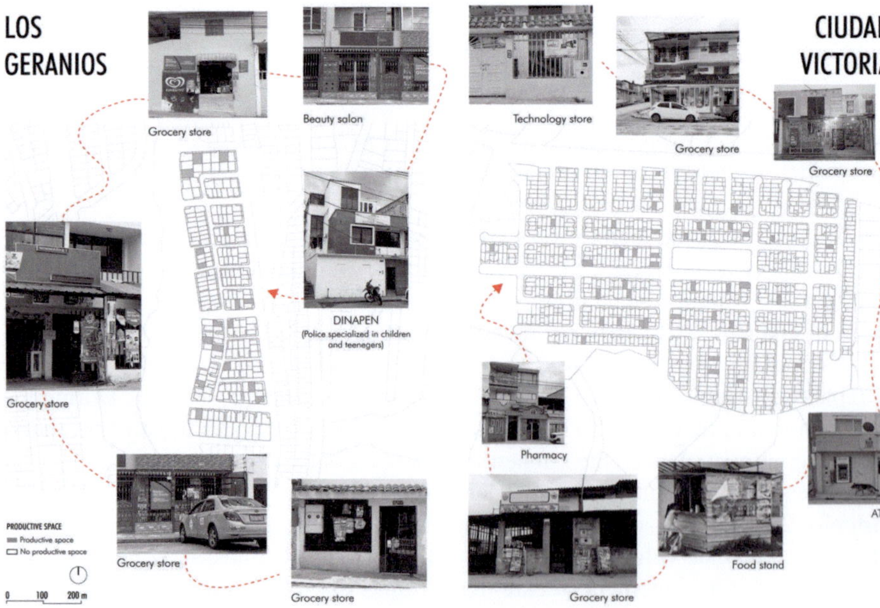

Fig. 7 The productive space integrated into the homes responds to microeconomies that arise to meet the economic needs of the neighborhood's residents

materials in roofs and façades, to improve wall finishes, to paint or build personalized enclosure walls, etc.; these alterations are undertaken either by seeking small financing loans or by using the family's savings. This is a strategy of distinction describing how indebted individuals try to differentiate themselves using cultural capital and consumption choices in order to improve their status and social position. This concept provides a critical perspective on social and cultural dynamics and has had a significant impact on contemporary sociology.

Interventions in the two neighborhoods analyzed in this study began within the first few years of home ownership. This criterion can also be used as an indication of dissatisfaction with the design; the greater the discontent, the greater the transformation. In other cases, the owner's interest is in the lot rather than the house; in this case, the building is replaced by a new one after 5 years. This begs a question: how is 'decent housing' perceived when the initial program does not respond to the specific needs of a household; in this case it helps to understand housing not as a finished product, but as an incremental process.

Housing transformations also extend to the socio-spatial configuration of the neighborhoods. It is possible to appreciate intentional and unintentional transformations. As regards intentional transformations, results showed there was a need to adapt communal spaces, which in the literature review have been identified as "units of spontaneous appropriation" (Bamba-Vicente 2020). The space with the greatest value is the sports space; neighbors have been willing to financially contribute to the intervention. Sports competitions are a way to achieve not only integration, but also obtain funds for social activities or minor works to improve the communal space.

In terms of unintentional transformations, the emphasis is on the morphology of the residential area and changes in use. By 'unintentional' we refer to the owner's omission of the impact on the block and neighborhood since these are deliberate transformations of the unit, even if individual alterations do not have a direct impact on the street structure or on public space.

Spatial adaptations and incremental modifications modify the initial socio-spatial densities and urban image of the dwellings that are transformed by changing the buildings' composition and layout. As a result, it is difficult to think of a logic governing the organization of the complex which, added to the lack of municipal regulations, triggers a precarious relationship between housing and the urban environment (Bustos Peñafiel 2014).

6 Conclusions

Ever since the genesis of the *VIS* programs the latter have involved families in a financial commitment which, paradoxically, is extended and renewed throughout the life of its beneficiaries, like a necessary evil that families try to avoid. This is obvious in the prepayment of mortgage debt; this behavior would appear to respond more to the fear of not being able to repay the debt should there be a future scenario of economic or labor instability, especially in a country such as Ecuador characterized by political and economic instability.

Prepayment is also evidence of payment facilities and capacity to pay. In the case of the Los Geranios neighborhood, the inhabitants received incentives through discounts, especially at Christmas, thus motivating the owners to prepay the debt. This is not the case with the "Ciudad Victoria" social housing program, which is part of a different housing policy, one in which the creditor is not the state but a private bank; the interest rate was fixed and in this case there were no incentives for prepayment. Nevertheless, some homeowners sought to pay off their debt in advance; this could call into question whether or not the selection of beneficiaries was fair, as these programs were designed for a middle class that may present several scenarios of need.

The analysis of the two case studies in Loja has shown that within 10 years 50% of the social housing was modified. The building setbacks have acted as a flexible space, compensating for the reduced land area; even municipal regulations have allowed it to be occupied. This explains why almost 50% of the front setbacks are occupied in "Los Geranios" where the plot was much smaller than in "Ciudad Victoria" where occupation of setbacks was less than 10%.

The need for flexible housing with regard to *VIS* is not a novelty, but putting it under the magnifying glass of financing allows us to question how these transformations should be planned so that they can be financed with savings and microcredits which, for different reasons discussed in this chapter, are preferable compared to large sum loans by financial institutions. The role of the state as a lender or facilitator of credit by private financial institutions should be further explored as a public policy, taking into account the advantages or disadvantages for the beneficiaries.

Moreover, the process of indebtedness of homeowners is a reflection of housing problems and restrictions, triggering considerations about the demand and supply policies inherent in the *VIS* programs. Changes to standard housing are inevitable; in some countries, such as Chile, this is already taken for granted: these transformations are expected and therefore social housing is designed and built based on the concept of a growing core (Aryani et al. 2015). It is crucial that from its initial conception, housing be designed as an adaptable system, prepared to face the inevitable alterations to which it will be subjected over a period of time. It is clear that new responses are required regarding the VIS as a social project, allowing for the appropriation and personalization of spaces, and taking into account the lifestyles and microeconomies that are exploited in housing, considered not only as a domestic habitat, but also as a productive space. Finally, consolidated *VIS* projects should not be considered from a planning point of view as a closed project, but should be continuously evaluated as an ecosystem that is constantly being financed.

6.1 Key Findings

Financialization and debt: *VIS* perpetuates a cycle of debt, forcing homeowners to seek additional loans or microcredits for essential home modifications.

Spatial transformations as a response to deficiencies: Many homes undergo modifications soon after acquisition due to the rigid and inadequate original designs.

Financial strategies for home modifications: Homeowners often prefer alternative financing sources, such as microcredits, remittances, or savings, over high-interest institutional loans.

Impact on neighborhood morphology: Between 50% and 90% of *VIS* dwellings in the study areas have been altered, leading to significant changes in neighborhood structures.

The need for flexible housing policies: Current *VIS* frameworks fail to incorporate flexibility in both design and financing, limiting their long-term sustainability.

Finally, urban planning regulations should be strengthened to avoid informal expansions that may compromise neighborhood infrastructure. Encouraging community-led housing models will empower residents, giving them greater control over their living environments.

Competing Interest The authors of this chapter declare that they have no financial, institutional, or personal conflicts of interest that could have influenced its selection, editing, or publication.

References

Acosta ME (2009) Políticas de vivienda en Ecuador desde la década de los 70: análisis, balance y aprendizajes [Master Thesis, FLACSO]. http://hdl.handle.net/10469/892

Acosta ME (2022) Mejorando vidas en Ecuador: Vivienda social inclusiva. Ciudades sostenibles, Banco interamericano de desarrollo. https://blogs.iadb.org/ciudades-sostenibles/es/mejorando-vidas-en-ecuador-vivienda-social-inclusiva#:~:text=Aunque%20ALC%20es%20la%20regi%C3%B3n,los%20hogares%20de%20menores%20ingresos. Accessed 23 June 2024

Alcívar Macías S, Cobos M, Forero Fuentes B (2018) Análisis funcional de la vivienda de interés social: El Recreo, cantón Durán 2017. Rev Conrado 14:99–104. https://conrado.ucf.edu.cu/index.php/conrado/article/view/628. Accessed 11 May 2023

Aranda Dioses E, Torres Caldas P (2023) La vivienda de interés social en ciudades intermedias del Perú Representaciones sociales y prácticas de innovación social. Rev Cien Soc 36:52. https://doi.org/10.26489/rvs.v36i52.6

Arnold P (2019) Políticas de producción y gestión social del hábitat en América Latina: conquistas de dere- chos e incidencia política frente a la "vivienda de interés social" orientada al mercado. In: Salinas Arreortua L (ed) Gestión urbana y política de vivienda. Espacio público, (in)seguridad y conflicto urbano. Ediciones Monosílabo, México, pp 225–260

Aryani S, Mulyadi M, Wahyuningsih IES (2015) The house design transformation: the preferences and the patterns. Procedia Environ Sci 28:717–724. https://doi.org/10.1016/j.proenv.2015.07.084

Bamba-Vicente JC (2020) Desplazamientos, alteraciones, subversiones: arquitectura de vivienda social y dimensiones de lo colectivo en la ciudad de Guayaquil. [Tesis (Doctoral), E.T.S]. Universidad Politécnica de Madrid

Baraya S (2020) El área mínima de vivienda: ¿Quién determina los espacios más pequeños permitidos en Latinoamérica? ArchDaily. https://www.archdaily.cl/cl/948641/el-area-minima-de-vivienda-quien-determina-los-espacios-mas-pequenos-permitidos-en-latinoamerica. Accessed 6 June 2023

Buckley RM, Kallergis A, Wainer L (2016) The emergence of large-scale housing programmes: beyond a public finance perspective. Habitat Int 54:199–209. https://doi.org/10.1016/j.habitatint.2015.11.022

Bustos Peñafiel M (2014) Condominios sociales como expresión de la masificación de vivienda colectiva (1976-2000). In: Vivienda social en copropiedad. Memoria de tipologías en condominios sociales, MIMPU, pp 317–410

Carrión F (1996) La penuria de la vivienda en el Ecuador. Fe Justicia 1:111–120. https://wwwflacsoandeseduec/agora/la-penuria-de-la-vivienda-en-el-ecuador Accesses 2 January 2024

Carvajal BC, Marín González F, Ibarra Morales L (2023) Triangulación de métodos en ciencias sociales como fundamento en la investigación universitaria en Latinoamérica. Mayéut Rev Cien Human Artes 11(2):43–58. https://doi.org/10.5281/zenodo.8140907

Cavallero L (2021) Hacia una definición de la violencia financiera. Rev Estud Polít Género 5:151–165. https://revistas.untref.edu.ar/index.php/ellugar/article/view/1026/839. Accessed 14 October 2023

Cavallero L, Gago V (2020) Endeudar para gobernar: sobre el extractivismo financiero hacia los sectores subalternos. Rev Invest CRONÍA 16(20):49–59

Córdova MA (2015) Transformación de las políticas de vivienda social. El Sistema de Incentivos para la Vivienda en la conformación de cuasi-mercados en Ecuador. Íconos. Rev Cien Soc 19(53):127–149. https://doi.org/10.17141/iconos.53.2015.1530

Datta K, Jones GA (2001) Housing and finance in developing countries: invisible issues on research and policy agendas. Habitat Int 25(3):333–357. https://doi.org/10.1016/S0197-3975(00)00038-2

Defensoria del Pueblo (2013) Informe annual 2013. https://www.defensordelpueblo.es/informe-anual/informe-anual-2013/. Accessed 2 July 2023

Delgadillo V (2018) Financiarización global de la vivienda: lucro y desplazamientos sociales. Econ Soc Territorio 18(57):621–627. https://doi.org/10.22136/est20181204

Demirgüç-Kunt A, Klapper L, Singer D, Ansar S (2022) The global findex database 2021. The World Bank, Washington. https://doi.org/10.1596/978-1-4648-1897-4

Durán G, Bayón M, Bonilla Mena A, Janoschka M (2020) Vivienda social en Ecuador: violencias y contestaciones en la producción progresista de periferias urbanas. Rev INVI 35(99):34–56. https://doi.org/10.4067/S0718-83582020000200034

García-Huidobro F, Torriti D, Tugas N (2010) PREVI Lima y la experiencia del tiempo. Rev Iberoamericana Urban 3:10–19

González Couret D, Párraga JFV (2019) Evolución de la vivienda de interés social en Portoviejo. Cuadernos Vivienda Urban 12:23. https://doi.org/10.11144/Javeriana.cvu12-23.evis

Greene M, González E (2011) Chile vivienda incremental: Una investigación del Banco Interamericano de Desarrollo. https://www.researchgate.net/publication 254422242_Chile_vivienda_incremental_Una_investigacion_del_Banco_Interamericano_de_Desarrollo. Accessed 12 March 2023

Guzmán-Ramírez A, Bravo-Patiño MÁ (2017) Estudio sobre las etapas de transformación en la Vivienda de Interés Social. Caso de estudio: Fraccionamiento "Valle De Los Naranjos" en la ciudad de Celaya, Guanajuato. Rev Legado Arquit Diseño 1:22. https:legadodearquitecturaydiseno.uaemex.mx/article/view/11348. Accessed 3 December 2023

Harker C (2021) Spacing debt obligations, violence, and endurance in Ramallah, Palestine, 1st edn. Duke University Press Books, Durham

Held G (2000) Políticas de viviendas de interés social orientadas al mercado: experiencias recientes con subsidios a la demanda en Chile, Costa Rica y Colombia. (Naciones U). CEPAL. https://www.cepal.org/sites/default/files/publication/files/5304/S00050485_es.pdf. Accessed 4 February 2024

Hermida MA, Cabrera N, Molina L (2019) Casas y Conjuntos. Vivienda social en Cuenca entre 1973 y 2014. Universidad de Cuenca, Cuenca

INEC (2022) VIII Censo de Población y VII de Vivienda. https://www.censoecuador.gob.ec/wp-content/uploads/2023/10/Presentación_Nacional_1°entrega-4.pdf. Accessed 7 June 2023

Link F, Señoret A, Figueroa C (2022) Del barrio al conjunto: Espacio público y sociabilidad en la vivienda social de Santiago. Rev INVI 37(106):49–72. https://doi.org/10.5354/0718-8358.2022.67125

Medialdea García B, Sanabria Martín A (2013) La financiarización de la economía mundial: hacia una caracterización. Rev Econ Mundial 32:195–227

Ministerio de Desarrollo Urbano y Vivienda (2013) Plan Nacional de Vivienda Social. https://www.habitatyvivienda.gob.ec/wp-content/uploads/downloads/2019/06/PROGRAMA-NACIONAL-DE-VIVIENDA-SOCIAL.pdf. Accessed 14 June 2024

Ministerio de Desarrollo Urbano y Vivienda (2018) Ecuador y la Nueva Agenda Urbana. Documento base. https://www.habitatyvivienda.gob.ec/wp-content/uploads/downloads/2019/01/AGENDA-URBANA-NACIONAL.pdf. Accessed 25 June 2023

Ministerio de Hábitat y Vivienda (2021) Deficit de Vivienda en Ecuador. https://www.habitatyvivienda.gob.ec/deficit-habitacional-nacional/. Accessed 11 April 2023

Molinatti F, Peláez E (2017) La localización como factor crítico. Análisis del programa "Mi Casa, Mi Vida". Córdoba, Argentina. Cuad Econ 36(71):521–548. https://doi.org/10.15446/cuad.econ.v36n71.55748

Municipio de Loja, UTPL, GIZ (2018) Laboratorio urbano de Loja 2018. Habitar la periferia (Cedrés, La). Editorial Universidad Técnica Particular de Loja, Loja. https://www.bivica.org/file/view/id/5845. Accessed 8 December 2023

Murillo S (2021) El déficit de vivienda en Ecuador, no solo es un problema numérico sino de calidad. El Telegrafo. https://www.eltelegrafo.com.ec/noticias/actualidad/44/deficit-vivienda-ecuador-problema-numerico-calidad. Accessed November 2023

OACDH (2010) El derecho humano a una vivienda adecuada. Oficina del Alto Comisionado de las Naciones Unidas para los Derechos Humanos. https://www.ohchr.org/sites/default/files/Documents/Publications/FS21_rev_1_Housing_sp.pdf

Ospina ÓR, Erazo Espinosa J (2009) Dolarización y generación de vivienda formal su lectura en Ecuador. Rev Ecuador Debate 76:29–53. http://repositorio.flacsoandes.edu.ec/handle/10469/4183. Accessed 8 August 2024

Partenio F (2022) Deudas, cuidados y vulnerabilidad: el caso de las mujeres de hogares de clases populares en la Argentina. Comisión Económica para América Latina y el Caribe (CEPAL) https://repositorio.cepal.org/server/api/core/bitstreams/c33bdf8c-5944-4302-a8a1-6d2bc65e6468/content. Accessed 12 December 2023

Peñaloza V, Paula Sousa FG, De Carvalho HA, Denegri Coria M (2019) Representaciones Sociales del endeudamiento del consumidor, diferencias por género, edad y grupos de renta. Polis 18(54):1406. https://doi.org/10.32735/S0718-6568/2019-N54-1406

Pérez A, González Couret D (2011) PREVI Lima y Elemental Chile. Lecciones aprendidas. Arqutect Urban 32(3):48–55. https://www.redalyc.org/pdf/3768/376839863007.pdf. Accessed 2 December 2023

Reglamento de Vivienda de Interés Social e Interés Público (2022). https://www.habitatyvivienda.gob.ec/wp-content/uploads/2022/04/Decreto_Ejecutivo_No._405.pdf. Accessed 21 May 2023

Rodas Beltrán AP (2013) La habitabilidad en la vivienda social en Ecuador a partir de la visión de la complejidad: elaboración de un sistema de análisis. Cuadernos Vivienda Urbanismo https://revistas.javeriana.edu.co/index.php/cvyu/article/view/5924. Accessed 2 April 2024

Rodríguez A, Sugranyes A (2009) El traje nuevo del emperador: las políticas de financiamiento de vivienda social en Santiago de Chile. https://biblioteca.clacso.edu.ar/clacso/gt/20120413123620/gthi1-2.pdf. Accessed 5 August 2023

Rolnik R (2021) La guerra de los lugares. La colonización de la tierra y la vivienda en la era de las finanzas. Editorial El Colectivo, Buenos Aires https://drive.google.com/file/d/1bbOXSsXUg9Q1gjBRQkmlocdfqGln4NIi/view. Accessed 4 January 2025

Ross A (2017) La creditocracia y los argumentos para resistirse al pago de las deudas. https://www.perlego.com/es/book/2564366/la-creditocracia-y-los-argumentos-para-resistirse-al-pago-de-las-deudas-pdf. Accessed 7 December 2023

Saldana J (2013) The coding manual for qualitative researchers, 2nd edn. SAGE, Washington. https://emotrab.ufba.br/wp-content/uploads/2020/09/Saldana-2013TheCodingManualforQualitativeResearchers.pdf. Accessed 25 April 2024

Thornton C (2024) Economía feminista y el Apocalipsis de la gente. In: Thornton C (ed) Holograma. Salud feminista entre pares pares para un futuro postcapitalista. Crater Invertido, Mexico, pp 100–114. https://d1wqtxts1xzle7.cloudfront.net/58583641/. Accessed 7 November 2024

Thornton C, Haiven M (2019) Economía feminista y Qué es la imaginación radical

Torres-Pérez ME, Arana-López G, Fernández-Martinez Y (2016) La calle y la vivienda: relaciones de espacio público y vida comunitaria. Quivera Rev Estud Territoriales 18(2):31–53. https://www.redalyc.org/journal/401/40152906003/html/. Accessed 17 August 2023

Vera F, Wainer SL (2018) Vivienda ¿Qué viene? Atributos para Re-Imaginar la vivienda de las próximas décadas. In: Adler V, Vera F (eds) Vivienda ¿Qué viene?: De pensar la unidad a construir la ciudad. Banco Interamericano de Desarrollo, Washington. https://catalogo.extension.cchc.cl/documentos/documentos/45108-2.pdf. Accessed 3 February 2023

Zumelzu-Scheel A (2016) Forma urbana y sostenibilidad: pasado, presente y desafíos. Una Rev 20:77–85. https://doi.org/10.4206/aus.2016.n20-12

Conclusions: Debt Spaces as "Burn Zones" Between Subjugation and Resistance Strategies

Antonio di Campli

Abstract This chapter examines debt as a pervasive force shaping contemporary urban life, particularly in Latin American contexts such as Ecuador. It explores how financial colonization and the intertwining of formal and informal debt have transformed housing into a site of both subjugation and resistance. The concept of "burn zones," inspired by Carla Benedetti, is used to describe the spaces where individuals and communities navigate the tensions between economic dependency and acts of defiance. The text highlights how debt not only dictates access to housing but also reshapes domesticity, gender roles, and urban infrastructures. Through an interdisciplinary approach, the research reveals how financialized urban spaces generate vulnerabilities but also foster collective strategies of resilience and opposition. Ultimately, the chapter argues for rethinking urban planning and architecture as political tools to challenge the exploitative dynamics of financialization and envision alternative modes of inhabiting.

Keywords Debt spaces · Financial colonization · Burn zones · Urban resistance

Debt has established itself as a shared experience, an omnipresent phenomenon permeating every aspect of contemporary life, intricately tied to the simultaneous unfolding of economic, social, and climate crises. In Ecuador, as in many other Latin American contexts, the expansion of individual and family indebtedness cannot be separated from the pervasive and opaque processes of financial colonization that have redefined popular habitats.

On the one hand, access to bank mortgages has tied middle- and lower-middle-income populations to long-term economic dependency circuits. On the other hand, informal debt has spread within the most fragile social fabrics, taking root in the lower classes. The interplay between formal and informal debt has thus created a complex system where the two dimensions feed into each other, generating a web of constraints that entrap everyday life.

A. di Campli (✉)
DIST, Interuniversity Department of Urban and Regional Studies and Planning, Politecnico di Torino, Torino, Torino, Italy
e-mail: antonio.dicampli@polito.it

A. di Campli (ed.), *Inhabiting Debt*, The Latin American Studies Book Series, https://doi.org/10.1007/978-3-031-99886-7_5

These processes, however, do not operate solely on the economic plane. They translate into spatial and material transformations that profoundly reorganize the existence of individuals, families, collectives, and urban communities. Building a house—a gesture meant to embody autonomy and rootedness—has instead become emblematic of a constant exposure to logics of control and subordination. In this context, concepts such as domesticity, protection, and care are no longer stable values but manipulable variables, rewritten according to the needs of an exploitative system.

The contemporary challenge, therefore, is not limited to observing how debt transforms space but also seeks to understand how this transformation affects the very meaning of life's reproduction. This dynamic particularly impacts women: custodians of domesticity, they are also the first to bear the brunt of the economic and social obligations imposed by debt.

An interdisciplinary approach has been necessary to explore these connections. Urban, social, economic, and feminist perspectives have contributed to deconstructing the dependency relationships between individuals, economies, and spaces, revealing their ambivalent nature. While these relationships create constraints, they also generate practices of resistance, often rooted in community solidarity and the collective capacity to imagine alternatives. In these strategies of resistance, the possibility lies in critically rethinking the relationship between the production of space and social reproduction. Therefore, urban and architectural design cannot be conceived as a neutral gesture but as a political act: a tool to oppose structural inequalities and envision new ways of inhabiting capable of challenging the logics of exploitation and global crises.

Debt spaces are therefore burn zones, spaces and situations where people or groups are exposed to risks or dangers, but at the same time can be points of resistance or struggle. These "zones" represent areas where the body and mind are tested, creating conflicts between the desire to submit to a dominant system and the drive to resist or rebel against it. The "burn zones" in Carla Benedetti's thought are rooted in a critical and complex analysis of the relationship between the individual and power. In these zones, the condition of vulnerability and exposure to risk is never simple or unilateral. They are spaces where the individual or group find themselves between two opposing forces: one that tends toward submission and one that promotes resistance. This duality creates a conflicted terrain where, although people are "burned" by external pressure, they can find moments of awareness and self-affirmation. Burn zones are not just places of suffering and domination, but can also be places of transformation, where suffering can generate critical consciousness and new models of resistance (Benedetti 2011).

Benedetti often uses this metaphor to reflect on the contradictions inherent in social, cultural, and economic contexts, where the individual is continuously tested by power dynamics that seem inevitable. The "burn" represents not only damage or injury, but also the opportunity for an "awakening," a reaction against injustice. It is, therefore, a concept that refers to a condition of no retreat: in these zones, the individual is forced to confront their own vulnerability and resistance in a way that does not offer easy escape, but can, at the same time, fuel new forms of struggle and liberation.

Recent studies on the financialization of housing (Salinas and Janoschka 2023) describe a profoundly transformed landscape, where housing is no longer merely a refuge but has become a crucial connector in the processes of capital accumulation. Once associated with protection and stability, the home is now deeply intertwined with global financial dynamics, becoming a commodity to be valued, traded, and mortgaged. Phenomena such as subprime lending, the unplanned expansion of urban peripheries (Reis and Lukas 2022), and the growing indebtedness of families—particularly those renting (Guerreiro et al. 2022)—draw a new geography of dwelling: fragmented, precarious, and marked by systemic vulnerabilities.

Within this context, feminist reflections (Cavallero and Gago 2019) have shifted attention to the lived experience of debt, revealing how it profoundly shapes personal and social relationships. In particular, housing debt is rooted in the labor of social reproduction (Federici 2014), amplifying burdens on women, who not only inhabit these precarious spaces but also sustain household economies and survival networks. Understanding financialization, therefore, requires not only analyzing its macroeconomic effects but also delving into its intimate and material consequences.

Yet, despite these contributions, few analyses have placed the home at the center of the debt crisis (Brickell et al. 2020). What is missing is a broader understanding of the multiple dependencies that arise—not only those between tenants and financial institutions but also those forged between neighbors, communities, and families through informal debt networks that shape housing spaces. Even less explored are the practices through which women, and communities more broadly, respond to this crisis: strategies of resistance and reconstruction that manifest in the reorganization of housing infrastructures and the reestablishment of communal relationships.

Our work situates itself within this perspective. We have investigated the nexus between debt and habitat, examining how debt relations—both formal and informal—shape spaces and infrastructures and how these, in turn, delineate new geographies of debt. Simultaneously, we have explored the interactions among the various actors involved: families, neighbors, banks, and mutual aid networks, showing how these relationships not only create constraints but also become grounds for resistance and social innovation.

The concept of "urban development financialization," which gained prominence after the 2008 financial crisis, now provides a valuable lens for understanding these phenomena. While rooted in broader processes of capital urbanization and neoliberal urban policies that have been reshaping cities for decades (Harvey 1985, 1989), it was with the collapse of the subprime mortgage market and the failure of Lehman Brothers that the relationship between economy, finance, and urban dwelling became explicit and central to disciplinary debates.

This crisis demonstrated that financialization does not merely shape real estate markets but reorganizes the very conditions of dwelling: spaces, social ties, and survival strategies. The home, once a safe haven, is now a financial asset, exposed to speculative logics, market fluctuations, and systemic precariousness. Yet, this transformation is not solely a source of vulnerability; it also prompts new forms of resistance and solidarity from the margins. Everyday practices of self-organization and mutual aid, often invisible, offer alternatives: strategies to inhabit and live in cities differently, constructing spaces that challenge the dominant logic and open up possibilities for the future. In this sense, the reflection on housing debt is not only a critique of the present but an opportunity to imagine the future: a future where the home is not a constraint but a possibility.

Debt is, for many, a daily experience, a factor that profoundly influences the ways of inhabiting and reproducing life, and that redefines the relationships of care and protection within domestic spaces. Today, the production of many living spaces is intrinsically linked to forms of debt that not only modify relationships within the home but also redefine social bonds and the traditional care and protection roles associated with the family domain. Debt thus becomes a condition that blurs the boundaries between the private and public spheres, helping to dissolve distinctions that, although historically established, now appear increasingly fragile and interconnected. It is, therefore, not an isolated phenomenon, but an interpretative key to understanding the ongoing transformations, not only in economic terms but also socially and urbanistically, within a context increasingly dominated by finance. In this context, the issue of debt is situated within the broader framework of the financialization of urban development, a process that reshapes not only the economy but also the social geography of cities. Debt, understood as an economic phenomenon, is an integral part of a larger system where finance emerges as a driving force for change, capable of shaping cities and turning them into investment markets. Financialization does not only act upon the production of housing but transforms its very logic of existence, generating new forms of inequality, creating economic dependence, and pushing for a redefinition of the relationships between people and urban space. What was once considered a necessity, the home, has now transformed into a financial asset to buy, sell, and speculate upon, where debt and its implications become an inescapable reality for millions of people.

The contemporary debate on the relationship between finance and cities revolves around three main areas of inquiry. The first concerns the financialization of residential housing (Fields and Uffer 2016; Aalbers 2016), where homes, once fundamental rights, have become financial commodities to be traded on markets, fueling a speculative spiral that directly impacts the lives of residents. The second area involves the growing role of digital platforms (Schwarz 2017; Shaw 2020; Fields 2022), which open new market spaces and avenues for interaction, while simultaneously strengthening the control of financial institutions over urban life. Finally, the third area addresses the pervasiveness of financialization processes, which not only affect the development of cities but extend to every corner of urban reality, making finance an increasingly influential player in the redefinition of the city as a social and political space (Alami and Dixon 2020; Aalbers 2022; Alami et al. 2022; Eagleton-Pierce 2023). Financialization, therefore, is no longer a localized phenomenon but has a transversal impact on every aspect of urban life, producing effects that are both invisible and deeply rooted.

Although most studies on the financialization of housing focus on cities like New York, London, and Hong Kong (Beswick et al. 2016; Fields 2017), where speculative processes are more evident, it is important to emphasize that these same dynamics are emerging in other cities, including those in Latin America, as well as in many other contexts that have been little explored by academic research. In these places, despite local differences, it is possible to trace the same patterns of financialization that, starting from the real estate market, permeate and profoundly alter the quality of life of residents. Thus, there is an urgent need to broaden the scope of research, not only to better understand the ongoing transformations but also to develop political and social responses that can effectively address the challenges posed by an increasingly invasive and determining financial capital in the future of our cities.

This volume aims to interrogate the transformation of Latin American urban spaces, revealing their deep connection to global economic and financial processes. By exploring the possibility that cities like Quito and Loja share similar dynamics with other urban realities worldwide, the approach taken seeks to highlight the links between economic, financial, and urbanization dynamics. But it goes further. It also aims to decipher the processes of financial colonization currently affecting popular habitats, viewed not only as physical places but also as symbolic spaces of contradictions and conflicts, where debt, in all its forms, plays a central role.

These processes, inherently complex, are not the result of a single cause or actor. On the contrary, they arise from the interaction of a plurality of subjects—not only developers and financial institutions but also real estate intermediaries, private owners, state apparatuses, and a broad and diverse population of residents, including migrants, who contribute to an ever-changing configuration. The variety of financial instruments used also reflects the diversity of interests at play, with individual actors operating according to their own logics, yet within a system that increasingly has a global dimension.

1 Resistance and Advocacy

The research develops on two distinct yet intertwined levels: on the one hand, analyzing how financial colonization shapes popular habitats; on the other, unveiling the effects of this transformation on the daily lives of individuals and communities. In both cases, the figure of debt—both formal and informal—becomes the thread that allows us to observe and understand the dynamics at play, outlining possible intervention paths. Debt is not merely an economic dimension: it is the interpretative key that enables the understanding of the new geometries of city and society.

The chapter entitled "Debt and Economic-Cultural Resilience in Social Housing Programs in Quito: The Carapungo and Solanda Neighborhoods" by Patricio Andino Sosa, David Pazmiño Amaya, and Rebeca Gallegos Bustamante examines the lived experiences of residents in the social housing projects of Solanda and Carapungo in Quito, Ecuador, highlighting how they developed cultural and economic resilience amidst systemic shortcomings. These communities faced complex challenges, including deficient infrastructure, limited public services, long-term debt, and adverse social conditions. Despite these difficulties, the residents employed collective strategies, cultural practices, and community-based leadership to improve their living conditions and create a sense of belonging and identity. The study reveals that the residents of these neighborhoods relied heavily on identity bonds to foster participatory democratic practices and collective leadership. This resilience manifested in organized community actions aimed at solving common problems and advocating for improvements in services and infrastructure. Women's collectives played a critical role, leading efforts to build support networks and strengthen social cohesion. These grassroots initiatives transformed the neighborhoods into spaces of collective struggle, enabling them to tackle adversity through cooperation and solidarity. The residents of Solanda and Carapungo utilized their cultural heritage and social knowledge as resources to navigate economic, political, and social pressures. By adapting their homes to accommodate future generations, they preserved cultural continuity while addressing practical needs. This approach reflected a deep commitment to their community's cultural and economic future, with homeownership representing both a significant burden and a powerful symbol of hope and achievement. The process of repaying long-term housing debt was seen as a journey of resilience, encompassing sacrifice, growth, and eventual empowerment. This struggle was not merely economic but also ideological, as it resisted the neoliberal state narrative that framed debt as an inevitable pathway to modernity and development. Residents rejected this imposed narrative by developing alternative ways of life grounded in their cultural values and collective knowledge. This act of resistance highlighted the residents' ability to challenge dominant systems and assert their cultural and economic agency. In their struggle for survival and dignity, the residents forged a unique "ecology of knowledge" that blended diverse cultural practices and grassroots experiences. This approach provided a framework for resisting state-driven and neoliberal impositions, emphasizing the community's capacity for innovation and resilience. By integrating non-Western and locally rooted knowledge, these neighborhoods developed effective strategies to overcome structural inequalities and systemic neglect. The case studies of Solanda and Carapungo illuminate the complex dynamics of cultural and economic resilience in the face of systemic neglect and neoliberal pressures. The residents' ability to organize, innovate, and resist highlights the transformative power of community solidarity and cultural heritage. However, the erosion of collective action and leadership in recent decades underscores the challenges of sustaining these gains over time. Even in the face of current difficulties, the enduring affection for their neighborhoods and the potential for renewed organization reflect the resilience and resourcefulness of these communities. This study stands out for its emphasis on cultural resilience, and community heritage; it offers a compelling narrative of resistance and adaptation, challenging dominant paradigms while affirming the value of community-based solutions.

The chapter entitled "This Never Ends: The Everlasting Conflict Between Debt, Spatial Growth, and Home Beautification in Solanda and Carapungo" by Andrea Pacheco Barzallo, Marco Lenin Lara Calderón, and Mauricio Unda Padilla delves into the complex interplay of debt, housing, and social dynamics in Quito, focusing on the social housing communities of Solanda and Carapungo. It demonstrates how debt operates not only as a financial mechanism but also as a transformative social and spatial practice. For families in these communities, the home is more than a physical structure; it is a living, evolving space shaped by the aspirations and sacrifices of multiple generations. Debt becomes an integral part of this process, enabling families to acquire and modify homes despite significant financial and emotional burdens. Ownership is seen as a shared familial achievement, transcending individual efforts to highlight the collective goal of creating a lasting legacy. This research explores how debt serves as a double-edged sword. While it facilitates access to homeownership and the expansion of living spaces, it also reinforces cycles of economic vulnerability. The interconnectedness of various debt forms—formal, informal, economic, and social—creates a web of obligations that impacts daily life. These debts do not exist in isolation but are deeply tied to the broader structures of global financial capitalism, which normalizes indebtedness as a necessary condition for participation in modern economic systems. In Quito, as in many other parts of the world, this dependency perpetuates poverty and exacerbates the marginalization of middle- and lower-income groups.

Spatial modifications in social housing are driven by the growing needs of families, particularly in multi-generational households. While these expansions offer solutions to immediate challenges, the lack of regulatory oversight often compromises structural safety and construction quality. The study underscores the importance of collaboration among governments, private sectors, and communities to address these issues. Governments must implement policies that support affordable and sustainable housing, while private-sector engagement and community involvement can ensure that expansions are both safe and functional. Such efforts require a holistic approach, integrating technical, economic, and social considerations to promote long-term stability and resilience.

The role of women in managing debt and household organization is a central theme of the study. Women often shoulder the dual burden of financial management and caregiving, making them key players in sustaining family economies. However, this dynamic also highlights the exploitative nature of financial systems, which capitalize on women’s unpaid and undervalued labor. The study critiques this exploitation, pointing to the broader link between women’s social roles and the vulnerabilities imposed by systemic indebtedness.

Debt is not merely a financial obligation; it is deeply embedded in the emotional and relational fabric of life. It affects intimate decisions, from mothers taking loans to secure their children’s futures to families forgoing basic needs to meet financial commitments. In Solanda and Carapungo, the pursuit of homeownership underpins this dynamic, with residents navigating systemic inequities while striving to create spaces of stability and dignity. This struggle highlights the resilience of these communities, which continue to adapt and resist despite the challenges they face.

This study critiques the broader economic and political systems that perpetuate debt dependency. Financial capitalism, driven by the endless production of debt, destabilizes social contracts and erodes trust in traditional systems of support. The normalization of debt as a condition of modern life—whether through mortgages, loans, or informal credit—ensures its perpetuation, often at the expense of those least equipped to bear its burdens. In Quito, the reliance on high-risk financial instruments exacerbates the impoverishment of vulnerable populations, creating a cycle of dependency that is difficult to escape.

Despite these systemic challenges, the study highlights the potential for resistance and advocacy. In Solanda and Carapungo, residents demonstrate a remarkable capacity for resilience and defiance, challenging the unjust structures that underpin their indebtedness. This resistance is rooted in a deep sense of community and shared purpose, which serves as a foundation for collective action. The study calls for systemic reforms to promote greater social, spatial, and economic justice. It advocates for policies that prioritize the needs of marginalized communities, ensuring access to affordable housing, safe living conditions, and equitable financial systems. Ultimately, this study paints a nuanced picture of debt in Quito, illustrating its dual role as both a tool for empowerment and a mechanism of exploitation. It emphasizes the need to reimagine economic systems that prioritize human dignity over financial gain. While debt remains a pervasive condition, the resilience and resistance of communities like Solanda and Carapungo offer hope for a more equitable and just future, where the pursuit of homeownership and stability is no longer tied to systemic oppression and sacrifice. This text adopts a broader a critical view, delving into the dynamics of debt as a financial, social, and emotional phenomenon, with particular attention to the role of women in economic management and family sustenance, exploring in detail the disproportionate burden placed on women, highlighting the exploitative nature of financial systems.

The chapter entitled "The Impact of Debt on the Transformation of Social Housing Programs in the City of Loja, Ecuador" by Andrea Ordoñez León, Claudia Costa-De los Reyes, Verónica Muñoz-Sotomayor, and María Fernanda León Vivanco, examines the dynamics of social housing in two Ecuadorian neighborhoods, Ciudad Victoria and Los Geranios, located in the city of Loja. The analysis focuses on the relationship between housing configurations, debt, and everyday life, capturing how the local population has reshaped their living spaces and communal areas in response to their needs, economic constraints, and social aspirations. By integrating both objective data and subjective experiences, the research sheds light on how spatial modifications and collective practices redefine the urban fabric.

In both neighborhoods, housing transformations were extensive, reflecting the inadequacy of the initial social housing program designs to accommodate the evolving needs of their inhabitants. In Ciudad Victoria, 47.3% of the dwellings were altered, while in Los Geranios, nearly all homes—92.8%—underwent modifications. These changes included adding new floors, occupying front setbacks, and renovating interiors, resulting in a departure from the uniformity of the original designs. Such unplanned interventions redefined the relationship between private and public spaces, often creating a hybrid use of spaces that merged domestic life with economic activities.

Productive spaces emerged as a significant feature of these transformations, particularly in Ciudad Victoria, where 7.7% of dwellings incorporated local businesses such as grocery stores, hair salons, and hardware shops. These additions addressed gaps in local infrastructure and services, especially in peripheral areas with limited access to urban amenities. In Los Geranios, 5.2% of homes included productive spaces, reflecting a lower demand due to better integration into the city and proximity to essential services. These spaces played a dual role, functioning as economic hubs and fostering a sense of community among residents.

Public and collective spaces were similarly reshaped through community efforts. In Ciudad Victoria, 32% of the total area was allocated to roads and pavements, with 18% designated as green areas, though these were not always accessible as public space. Residents compensated by organizing community events and funding improvements to create sports areas and recreational spaces. Los Geranios, with only 0.15% of its area allocated to public space, relied on the nearby linear park to fulfill recreational needs. In both neighborhoods, residents transformed sports areas and other communal spaces into vibrant hubs of activity, strengthening neighborhood cohesion and creating a sense of belonging.

Debt emerged as a central theme in this study, influencing both the configuration of housing and the living conditions of the residents. The initial financial burden of acquiring *VIS* housing (*vivienda de interés social* or social housing programs) was compounded by additional expenses for modifications to improve habitability. Many families took on further debt to address inadequacies in the original designs, such as minimal spaces, poor finishing, and lack of flexibility for future changes. These alterations, often carried out without technical supervision, included expanding living spaces, adding productive areas, and upgrading finishes to reflect personal preferences or display social status.

This study highlights the inadequacy of the original social housing designs, which were rigid and failed to anticipate the diverse and evolving needs of residents. Housing was initially conceived for nuclear families with medium-low incomes, but the designs did not account for larger family sizes or the necessity of incremental changes. As a result, dissatisfaction with the initial designs led to widespread modifications within the first few years of ownership. In some cases, the dissatisfaction was so profound that families abandoned their homes, further exacerbating challenges in these neighborhoods.

Despite these challenges, strong community bonds were evident in both Ciudad Victoria and Los Geranios. Residents actively engaged in communal activities and sports, which fostered integration and a sense of belonging. This was particularly significant given the infrastructural shortcomings, such as remoteness, limited public transportation, and poor-quality facilities. In Ciudad Victoria, for instance, commuting to the city center could take up to 40 min, with residents relying on private vehicles or motorcycles to navigate the inadequate public transport system.

This study concludes that social housing projects need to transition from static, pre-designed models to adaptable systems capable of evolving with the needs of their inhabitants. Housing should be viewed not as a finished product but as a process of incremental transformation. Financing mechanisms, including microcredits and savings-based models, should support these changes, reducing the reliance on high-interest loans. Moreover, the role of the state as a facilitator of credit or provider of incentives must be reconsidered to ensure fair access and long-term sustainability.

In addressing the socio-spatial dynamics of social housing programs, the necessity of participatory planning that incorporates the lived experiences of residents is underscored, advocating for the design of flexible housing systems that allow for personalization and appropriation while fostering the economic and social vitality of neighborhoods. Such an approach would not only improve the quality of life for residents but also ensure that social housing projects evolve as dynamic ecosystems responsive to the complex realities of urban life. This chapter focuses primarily on the technical and spatial aspects of housing transformations, with an explicit objective and quantitative perspective.

All the investigations and critical reflections presented in this volume share a series of common themes, while also highlighting some significant divergences. First and foremost, it is clear that all emphasize the resilience of social housing communities in addressing economic, social, and infrastructural challenges. Families living in these areas not only transform their living spaces to meet their needs but also use cultural practices and collective strategies to improve their living conditions. The chapter by Andino et al. highlights how resilience is expressed through participatory democratic practices and collective leadership. The chapter by Lara Calderón et al. explores debt management and spatial modifications as expressions of familial sacrifice and adaptability, emphasizing the social and symbolic significance of homeownership while the chapter by Ordoñez et al. focuses on the reorganization of living and communal spaces, showing how these changes reflect the adaptation to the needs of families.

Another shared central theme is the role of debt, which emerges as a structuring element in the life dynamics of these communities. Debt is described as both a tool for accessing homeownership and a burden that perpetuates economic vulnerability. In the first text, debt represents an ideological challenge against neoliberal narratives that present it as an inevitable path to development, while the second text directly links debt to the spatial transformations required to meet family needs. In the third text, debt is analyzed in a more complex manner, seen both as an opportunity and as an exploitation mechanism, highlighting its emotional and relational impact within families.

A further common element across the three studies is the focus on the transformations of living and communal spaces. These changes are a response to the housing and economic needs of families but also reflect the desire to adapt spaces to a more personal and functional vision. In the first text, transformed homes take on symbolic value as expressions of cultural continuity and resistance. In the second text, these transformations are analyzed in more technical detail, showing how they address the shortcomings of the original designs. The third text, finally, emphasizes the need to regulate such changes to ensure safety and sustainability, proposing a collaborative approach between the state, private sectors, and communities.

In summary, all the reflections share an emphasis on community tenacity and perseverance, on the role of debt, and the adaptation of dwelling spaces, but diverge in some analytical approaches and the emphasis on various aspects of social, economic, and cultural dynamics. The differences in perspective enrich the understanding of the complex realities of social housing communities in Ecuador, offering a multifaceted view of their strategies for adaptation and resistance in the face of challenges imposed by dominant economic and political systems.

2 Flexibility and Redundancy

Addressing the issue of debt through an urbanistic lens means examining how it not only conditions urban spaces but also transforms them into a terrain of inequality, precariousness, and exploitation. This process simultaneously involves the creation of spaces of resistance and opportunity. In this context, it is necessary to rethink the relationship between finance, habitation, and socio-spatial justice, to produce a new collective vision and course of action that breaks the dominant dynamics. Contemporary architecture and urban planning are thus called upon to respond to the structural inequalities created by financialization, designing spaces that are not merely responses to consumption-driven logic, but that contribute to a project of equity and social justice.

This evolving understanding of architecture and urban planning and design as a relational practice opens the door to designing spaces that engage with the economic and social dynamics, such as the financialization of urban environments, that demand new approaches to equity and justice.

Traditionally architecture has been concerned with the creation of objects—buildings. Hence the preoccupation was always the definition of forms. In recent times it was the advent of digital design that underscored the centrality of form creation. More significantly, creativity was linked to innovative form creation. While form creation is still necessary, it is now clear that architecture and urban planning and design—even when identified with objects and their assemblage—occur within logics that define the activity of building. Those logics include the logic of capital, of finance and the logic of carbon. But it is possible to trace the development of the identification of architecture with building to the possibility of rethinking architecture and urban planning and design after the centrality of the object. In other words, to think the development of relational architecture.

This shift toward a "relational architecture," which takes into account broader dynamics of capital, finance, and sustainability, directly connects to the concept of architectural flexibility conceived not just as a rejection to predetermined functions but as an opportunity for ongoing adaptation and transformation of spaces. In this view, architecture is no longer limited to formal staticity but becomes a dynamic entity that evolves over time, accommodating unforeseen, sometimes contradictory uses, and responding more fluidly to the changing needs of communities. The idea of surplus and flexibility, therefore, not only fosters the diversity of functions but also becomes a tool for addressing the complex socio-political and ecological challenges of today, where architecture must adapt to changes in social structures, economic dynamics, and environmental concerns without being constrained by a rigid, pre-established form.

Adrian 40 views flexibility in architecture not merely as designing spaces to serve a particular function but as incorporating extra capacity into the built environment, enabling these spaces to accommodate a variety of unforeseen uses over time. Historical examples, like baroque palaces or panopticon-style prisons, show how flexibility can emerge from abundant space, which allows the buildings to be adapted for different activities, sometimes even remaining unused in parts. Forty defines this as "flexibility through redundancy," emphasizing the creation of surplus capacity that opens the door for various interpretations and uses to evolve.

In architectural terms, flexibility arises from the inclusion of surplus space or "margins," which facilitates diverse, unpredictable, and at times even contradictory uses. This concept of redundancy contrasts with modern architecture, which often focuses on a strict, function-driven design where form is directly linked to purpose. Forty also argues that flexibility does not grant individuals more freedom in how they organize spaces but instead increases the degree of control that can be exercised over a project as it evolves. Flexibility, when seen as a political strategy, involves the liberation from conventional methods of control and domination. It highlights the ways in which users of a building appropriate and adapt existing structures, implementing flexible and multifunctional elements to satisfy the needs of a community. This broader understanding of architectural flexibility encompasses both the physical adaptability of spaces and the socio-political effects of how these spaces are utilized and transformed.

Therefore, "flexibility as redundancy" is not about anticipating every potential change, but rather about deliberately allowing for surplus space that accommodates unexpected, diverse, and occasionally conflicting and opposing uses (Forty 2000, pp. 142–149).

Debt spaces as "burn zones" become a way to describe the dialectical nature of subalternity and resistance: in such spaces, one is never completely dominated or completely free, but always oscillating between oppression and the possibility of antagonism. Burn zones are liminal, ambivalent areas full of potential: they are places where the body and mind confront the dominant system, but also places where resistance, awareness, and, ultimately, the possibility of transforming the system itself are born.

Every "burn" subject, space, ecology, becomes a place of a potential reaction, a new form of subjectivity that, even in pain, seeks to emerge.

All this research has tried to reason around these possibilities.

Competing Interest The author of this chapter declares that he has no financial, institutional, or personal conflicts of interest that could have influenced is selection, editing, or publication.

References

Aalbers M (2016) The financialization of housing. A political economy approach. Routledge, New York

Aalbers M (2022) State/finance symbiosis. Urban Geogr 44(4):1–7

Alami I, Dixon A (2020) State capitalism(s) redux? Theories, tensions, controversies. Compet Change 24(1):70–94

Alami I, Dixon A, Gonzalez-Vicene R et al (2022) Geopolitics and the 'new' state capitalism. Geopolitics 27:995–1023

Benedetti C (2011) Disumane lettere. Indagini sulla cultura della nostra epoca. Laterza, Bari

Beswick J, Alexandri G, Byrne M, Vives-Miró S, Fields D, Stuart Hodkinson S, Janoschka M (2016) Speculating on London's housing future. City 20(2):321–323

Brickell K, Picchioni F, Natarajan N, Guermond V, Parsons L, Zanello G, Bateman M (2020) Compounding crises of social reproduction: microfinance, over-indebtedness and the COVID-19 pandemic. World Dev 136:1–4

Cavallero L, Gago V (2019) Una lectura feminista de la deuda. ¡Vivas, libres y desendeudadas nos queremos! Rosa Luxemburg Foundation, Buenos Aires

Eagleton-Pierce M (2023) Uncovering the City of London corporation: territory and temporalities in the new state capitalism. Environ Plan A 55(1):184–200

Federici S (2014) From commoning to debt: Financialization, microcredit, and the changing architecture of capital accumulation, South Atlantic Quarterly 113(2):231–244

Fields D (2017) Urban struggles with financialization. Geogr Compass 11:11

Fields D (2022) Automated landlord: digital technologies and post-crisis financial accumulation. Environ Plann A Econ Space 54(1):160–181

Fields D, Uffer U (2016) The financialisation of rental housing. Urban Stud 53(7):1486–1502

Forty A (2000) Words and buildings: a vocabulary of modern architecture. Thames & Hudson, New York

Guerreiro I, Rolnik R, Marin-Toro A (2022) Neoliberal management of precarity: rental housing as a new neoliberal frontier of housing financialization. Cadernos Metrópole 24(54):451–476

Harvey D (1985) The urbanization of capital: studies in the history and theory of capitalist urbanization. Johns Hopkins University Press, Baltimore

Harvey D (1989) From managerialism to entrepreneurialism: the transformation in urban governance in late capitalism. Geogr Ann Ser B Hum Geogr 71(1):3–17

Reis N, Lukas M (2022) Beyond the megacity: new dimensions of peripheral urbanization in Latin America. University of Toronto Press, Toronto

Salinas LA, Janoschka M (2023) Las biopolíticas de la financiarización de la vivienda: una aproximación a las violencias epistémicas del capitalismo financiero. Rev Estud Soc 85:59–75

Schwarz JA (2017) Platform logic: an interdisciplinary approach to the platform-based economy. Policy Internet 9(4):374–394

Shaw J (2020) Platform real estate: theory and practice of new urban real estate markets. Urban Geogr 41(8):1037–1064

MIX
Papier aus verantwortungsvollen Quellen
Paper from responsible sources
FSC® C105338

If you have any concerns about our products,
you can contact us on
ProductSafety@springernature.com

In case Publisher is established outside the EU,
the EU authorized representative is:
Springer Nature Customer Service Center GmbH
Europaplatz 3, 69115 Heidelberg, Germany

Printed by Libri Plureos GmbH
in Hamburg, Germany